P9-CEU-636

FORMER
SOVIET
REPUBLICS

UKRAINE

BY LAUREL CORONA

LUCENT BOOKS
P.O. BOX 289011
SAN DIEGO, CA 92198-9011

TITLES IN THE FORMER SOVIET REPUBLICS SERIES INCLUDE:

The Baltics
The Central Asian States
The Russian Federation
The Transcaucasus
Ukraine

Library of Congress Cataloging-in-Publication Data

Corona, Laurel, 1949–
  Ukraine / by Laurel Corona.
    p. cm. — (Modern nations of the world)
Includes bibliographical references and index.
  ISBN 1-56006-737-3
  1. Ukraine—History—Juvenile literature. [1. Ukraine—History.]
I. Title. II. Series.
  DK508.515 .C67 2001
  947.7—dc21

00-011399

No part of this book may be reproduced or used in any form or by any means, electrical, mechanical, or otherwise, including, but not limited to, photocopy, recording, or any information storage and retrieval system, without prior written permission from the publisher.

Copyright © 2001 by Lucent Books, Inc.
P.O. Box 289011, San Diego, CA 92198-9011
Printed in the U.S.A.

CONTENTS

FOREWORD

THE CURTAIN RISES

Through most of the last century, the world was widely perceived as divided into two realms separated by what British prime minister Winston Churchill once called the "iron curtain." This curtain was, of course, not really made of iron, but of ideas and values. Countries to the west of this symbolic curtain, including the United States, were democracies founded upon the economic principles of capitalism. To the east, in the Soviet Union, a new social and economic order known as communism prevailed. The United States and the Soviet Union were locked for much of the twentieth century in a struggle for military, economic, and political dominance around the world.

But the Soviet Union could not sustain its own weight, burdened as it was by a hugely inefficient centralized government bureaucracy, by long-term neglect of domestic needs in favor of spending untold billions on the military, and by the systematic repression of thought and expression among its citizens. For years the military and internal police apparatus had held together the Soviet Union's diverse peoples. But even these entities could not overcome the corruption, the inefficiency, and the inability of the Communist system to provide the basic necessities for the Soviet people.

The unrest that signaled the beginning of the end for the Soviet Union began in the satellite countries of Eastern Europe in 1988—in East Germany, followed by Hungary, and Poland. By 1990, the independence movement had moved closer to the Soviet heartland. Lithuania became the first Baltic nation to declare its independence. By December 1991, all fifteen union republics— Armenia, Azerbaijan, Belarus, Estonia, Georgia, Kazakhstan, Kyrgyzstan, Latvia, Lithuania, Moldova, Russia, Tajikistan, Turkmenistan, Ukraine, Uzbekistan—had done the same. The Soviet Union had officially ceased to exist.

Today the people of new nations such as Uzbekistan, Latvia, Belarus, Georgia, Ukraine, and Russia itself (still the largest nation on earth) must deal with the loss of the certainties of the Soviet era and face the new economic and social challenges of the present. The fact that many of these regions have little if any history of self-governance adds to the problem. For better or worse, many social problems were kept in check by a powerful government during the Soviet era, and long-standing cultural, ethnic, and other tensions are once again threatening to tear apart these new and fragile nations. Whether these regions make an effective transition to a market economy based on capitalism and resolves their internal economic crises by becoming vital and successful participants in world trade; whether their social crises push them back in the direction of dictatorship or civil war, or move them toward greater political, ethnic, and religious tolerance; and perhaps most important of all, whether average citizens can come to believe in their own ability to improve their lives and their own power to create a government and a nation of laws that works in their own best

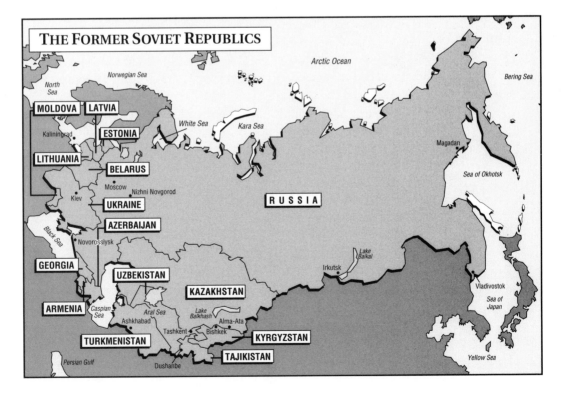

interests, are questions that the entire world, not just former Soviet citizens are pondering.

Sociologists and political scientists alike point to instability in the former Soviet republics as a serious threat to world peace and the balance of global power, and therefore it is more important than ever to be accurately informed about this politically and economically critical part of the world. With Modern Nations: Former Soviet Republics, Lucent Books provides information about the people and recent history of the former Soviet republics, with an emphasis on those aspects of their culture, history, and current situation that seem most likely to play a role in the future course of each of these new nations emerging from the shadows of the now vanished iron curtain.

INTRODUCTION

THE BEWILDERED GIANT

Ukraine is the largest country entirely within Europe, as opposed to being, like Russia, partly in Central Asia. Its strategic location between Russia and Western Europe and on the Black Sea, as well as its vast mineral and agricultural resources, made it a prized possession of the former Soviet Union. Thus, Ukraine's 1991 declaration of independence was a key factor in the collapse of what was once one of the most powerful countries in the world. Many observers speculated that Ukraine would be the showcase success story for a former Soviet republic's transition from communism to a Western-style democracy and economy. But despite now having claimed their country's resources and strengths for themselves, in the decade since independence the Ukrainian people have faced challenges in some respects more daunting than those faced by any other formerly Communist country, and today the country is still far from being the success story much of the world had hoped for.

A DISPUTED NEW IDENTITY

Today's Ukraine is deeply divided culturally. One of the present challenges is to establish a sense of national identity and common purpose, to create among all citizens a view that they are—and indeed want to be—"Ukrainian." For centuries Ukraine was perceived by the tsars, the former rulers of the Russian Empire, as Russian territory. To them, "the Ukraine" was only a region (as we might in the United States today refer to "the Southwest") despite the fact that the region had its own language and indigenous people. The tsars wanted to "Russify" the Ukrainian people, to make the Ukrainians see themselves as Russians, and over time they succeeded. In fact, many citizens of today's Ukraine feel a stronger identity as Russians than they do as Ukrainians. This cultural identification is so strong that even though the people of Ukraine overwhelmingly favored independence from the Soviet Union, the notion of cutting ties with what many perceive as their historical and cultural motherland, Russia, is not what many of them had in mind.

Others, however, see just such a breaking of ties as essential to establishing a separate national identity. These Ukrainians do not make a distinction between Russia, a centuries-old empire dominated by ethnic Russians, and the Soviet Union, a Communist entity that was in power in Russia and surrounding regions during most of the twentieth century. To them, Russia is responsible for centuries of oppression designed not just to break the spirit and culture of the Ukrainian people but to break their backs as well. These Ukrainians, often lumped together under the name "Ukrainian nationalists," want as little to do with Russia as possible. This divisiveness about Ukraine's identity in relation to Russia has created immense controversy and feelings of disunity just when unity is most needed.

Despite ten years of independence, many Ukrainians still view themselves as Russians.

REVIVING THE LANGUAGE

The first element of national identity, to many Ukrainians, is language. During the Soviet era, Russian was the only language

permitted in the workplace and in schools. Though peasants and other older Ukrainians still spoke Ukrainian at home, it was sneered at as quaint by many of the younger generation, and by all in authority. Ukrainian writers had to write in Russian to be published; those who deviated, such as poet Vasyl Stus, were sent by Communist authorities to remote arctic labor camps known as gulags, where they died of starvation and overwork. By the last few decades of the twentieth century, according to writer Ania Savage, "the demise of Ukrainian in Ukraine was not yet an accomplished fact, but it was a possibility. Russification had finally taken hold, and Ukraine, as a distinct nation, was dying."[1]

It is little wonder, then, that Ukrainian nationalists see reviving Ukrainian as essential to creating a national identity. However, this is no easy task. Many ethnic Ukrainians do not speak the language. Some wish to learn, but others do not see the point because Russian is perfectly adequate as a means of communication. Even though Ukrainian is now the official language in schools, there is little way to enforce its use. Many teachers do not speak it well, and many textbooks are still in Russian. Furthermore, some people feel that forcing the language of one

Although Ukrainian is the official language in the schools and in government, most of the population still speaks Russian.

ethnic group on the entire nation is just as repressive as forcing Russian on the region had been originally. Today a compromise has been reached: Ukrainian is used in schools and government, and Russian is recognized as a second official language by the nation's constitution.

A CULTURE RECLAIMED OR INVENTED?

This one example of conflict over language illustrates the kind of challenges that lie ahead as Ukraine struggles to build a strong national identity. Not just language but even the nation's history itself is a source of controversy. Ukrainians take great pride in those chapters of their history that make them seem fiercely committed to independence and the preservation of their unique culture, but the truth is that more powerful and better organized empires, most notably Russia (later the Soviet Union) and Poland, have controlled Ukraine for centuries. Today, history books are being rewritten to focus on people and events that showed resistance to such domination, but many Ukrainians feel this new version presents a false picture of the past.

Likewise, for centuries Ukrainians were taught to see the literary and artistic heritage of Russia as their own. Many Ukrainians see Russian writers such as Leo Tolstoy and composers like Pyotr Tchaikovsky as part of their own artistic heritage. Given that Ukrainian writers had to write in Russian if they wished to be published and dared not be too controversial on issues of Ukrainian identity and nationality, there are not many Ukrainian writers whose rediscovery could be helpful in building a sense of national artistic heritage today. Taras Shevchenko, a good nineteenth-century author but one whose works are not really in the same league as Tolstoy's *War and Peace*, has been brought to the forefront of school curriculum, but to some this seems yet another example of misguided efforts to make Ukraine seem more historically and culturally separate than it really is. There does not seem to be any easy compromise between those who bristle at calling their Russian oppressors part of their own heritage and those who are unwilling to participate in what they perceive as a contrived national identity.

A DECADE OF DISAPPOINTMENTS

It is little wonder then, in the face of such fundamental disagreements on what it means to be Ukrainian, that the country has had difficulty making an orderly transition into an independent nation. It has tried to accomplish several changes at once. The first is to build a national identity. The second is to build a functioning government, a nation ruled by laws. The third is to make the transition from a Communist to a capitalist economy, from a world where money was relatively unimportant in daily life to one where having or not having money affects nearly everything. These last two, creating a government of laws and a functioning economy, go hand in hand. There is no reliable system to ensure that people are paid fairly or at all, or to collect taxes to keep the government functioning. Financial crimes, ranging from leaders stealing from the treasury to thugs stealing money and property from ordinary citizens, are common today, and no police or court system has much effect. In fact, taking bribes is so rampant that often police and other legal authorities are part of the problem rather than the solution.

The thrilling times right after independence, when people believed that they would be able, through their own efforts, to make a better life for themselves and their families, have

After so many years under communism, Ukraine is finding it difficult to make the transition to a capitalist economy.

faded. Suddenly forced to take responsibility for their own lives, many found they did not know how. In a recent survey, almost three-quarters of Ukrainians said it was the state's responsibility to protect them from economic difficulty. When asked what democracy meant to them, 43 percent said freedom, but only 4 percent said personal responsibility. Though no one really wants the Soviet Union back, many still think communism is a better system for the Ukrainian people.

AN UNCERTAIN FUTURE

Ania Savage, an American reporter of Ukrainian descent who found herself in Kiev (the capital of Ukraine) when independence was declared, describes a statue of Soviet hero Lenin being taken down piece by piece while a crowd watches:

> Lenin is now losing an arm, now a piece of his flapping overcoat, [while] politics and history dominate the discourse. I find myself joining a group of passersby who have paused to listen to an impassioned orator. Everyone wants to examine the past and understand it. The rising voices carry such an intensity that you must stop and listen. People are publicly articulating their stories for the first time in their lives. As I join in the knots of people talking, arguing, listening, I don't get a sense of individuals telling individual stories but of many people telling the same story. The dams of silence are crumbling, as is the statue of Lenin across the street. The hum that rises above the street, above Kiev itself, is that of newfound voices, or recovered memories, of eagerness to search for understanding and to understand. The orators in the Square of Independence are recovering their—and Ukraine's—history.[2]

Much of that enthusiasm has by now turned to cynicism, anger, and regret for a past now painted far rosier than it really was. It is more unclear than ever whether Ukraine will be able to find its feet. Essential, of course, is to create a political and economic system that has the support of the majority of citizens regardless of their ethnic or cultural background. The enemy at this point seems to be time, for the chaos of present-day Ukraine cannot continue. But Ukraine has significant strengths as well, most notably its remarkable people, who show through crisis after crisis an unwillingness to give up, an absolute refusal to be bowed by the difficulties they face.

The Land and People of Ukraine

Despite its large size, Ukraine is not characterized by particularly great diversity in its geography. Instead, what is most noticeable about Ukraine are the vast stretches of similar scenery—its endless golden fields of grain; its vast, dark forests; its miles of coast; its dismal, ecologically ruined industrial valleys. Ukraine does have distinct regions, but these are in many cases as much a matter of history and culture as they are the lay of the land. Geographically the country changes from north to south, and historically and culturally it changes from west to east. Whatever approach one takes, it is apparent that Ukraine is a rich country, including the most precious resource of all, its people.

The Geography of Ukraine

Ukraine shares borders in its north and northwest with Belarus and Poland. Both southern Belarus and northwestern Ukraine are characterized by wet and often swampy forestland. To the west, Ukraine forms a bulge along its border with Poland, Slovakia, Hungary, and Romania. The provinces of Ukraine along the Polish border are known as Volhynia and Galicia, charming regions of small, picturesque villages and farms.

East of Galicia lies central Ukraine. Geographers call the terrain of this area a "wooded steppe," a grassy plain region punctuated by stretches of forest. The land is broken up by many small rivers, which have cut canyons and river basins over eons. The forests, at least those that remain after decades of poor conservation practices and extensive clear-cutting of lumber, are primarily located in the river valleys. Rain and snowfall provide sufficient water for extensive cultivation of crops on the plateaus. Typical crops of this region include sugar beets and sunflowers, grown for oil and seed.

The Ukrainian steppe is one of the richest agricultural regions in the world.

The term *wooded steppe* is a way of distinguishing a particular terrain from that of a true steppe, which is not usually wooded but a broad open plain. South of the wooded steppe of central Ukraine lies the true steppe region. Most people's associations with Ukraine are of the steppe, characterized as the breadbasket of the entire region. Lower in elevation than the wooded steppe, it is characterized by black soil known as *chernozem*. It is one of the richest agricultural regions of the world, capable of growing enough wheat and other grains to feed most of the former Soviet Union, although due to poor production strategies it failed to do so. The steppe stretches all the way to the Black Sea.

The vast majority of Ukraine's territory lies in the agricultural regions of the central wooded steppe and southern steppe region. One other region to the east also plays a central economic role in today's Ukraine. The Donetsk Basin, also called the Donbass, is rich in minerals, metals, and coal, and thus has become a center of heavy industry. Coal reserves in the basin are estimated at 90 billion tons. Iron and manganese deposits are also among the world's largest. Petroleum and natural gas reserves have been found in the region, as have profitable supplies of salt, mercury, and other valuable minerals and metals.

Two other geographic regions complete the territory of Ukraine. The first of these, the Crimean Peninsula, juts deep into the Black Sea and forms the southernmost region of Ukraine. Almost an island, it is anchored to Ukraine to the north and Russia to the east by thin strips of land, or isthmuses. The peninsula separates off a large portion of the Black Sea into the separate body of water known as the Sea of Azov. Crimea is a beautiful region, with a fabled coastal strip of beautiful resorts and an interior made up of one of the few true mountain ranges in all of Ukraine. The resort city of Yalta and the port of Sevastopol are both in Crimea. Sevastopol was considered so essential to the Soviet Union's defense that until 1996 no one, including residents, could enter or leave without special military clearance.

The final distinct region of Ukraine lies in its far west, where the Carpathian mountains, the second largest mountain range in Europe after the Alps, begin their rise over the Ukrainian border into Romania. This region, known generally as Transcarpathia, is a picturesque area characterized by evergreen forested mountains rising as high as six thousand feet, beautiful meadows and pastures, and narrow, twisting river valleys.

Although transportation networks in the region have lessened its remote character, Transcarpathia is still quite distinct from the rest of Ukraine, not just geographically but also historically and culturally.

THE CITIES OF UKRAINE

Scattered around Ukraine are the half dozen major cities that serve as focal points for the various regions of the country. Of the approximately 49 million people in Ukraine, though, only between 8 and 9 million live in the six largest cities combined, revealing that, for most Ukrainians, smaller cities and towns are home. However, these six cities—and many smaller ones all over Ukraine—have played and continue to play a large role in the political life of the country, and thus are key to its transition into a modern, independent nation.

KIEV

Kiev (Kyiv in Ukrainian) is not only the capital and largest city, with 2.6 million inhabitants, but also the most significant city historically. The first great historical era of the eastern Slavs, which include today's Russians and Belarusans as well as Ukrainians, began in what is known as Kievan Rus. This civilization, centered around Kiev, reached its peak in the ninth through eleventh centuries. The city was guarded by strong earthen walls, pierced by elaborately decorated gates that have survived in popular imagination as wonders of a past civilization even though they were destroyed in the twelfth century by the Mongols.

Today's Kiev is a chaotic place, symbolic of the lawlessness and confusion that characterize life in former Soviet countries. Little of the glory of the past remains except the interior mosaics and glittering exterior domes of beautiful St. Sophia's Cathedral, built in the eleventh century, and the fascinating Pechersky Caves Monastery, built over the centuries from its humble origins as cave dwellings and burial sites of monks into a huge religious complex. Another interesting site is the multi-colored eighteenth-century St. Andrew's Church, situated above the Podil, the historic merchant's district of Kiev. Ukraine's most important writer, Taras Shevchenko, is honored in the city's major park, Shevchenko Park, which is ringed by many of the most important museums of the city as well as buildings of the University of Kiev. These sites are sources of

Kiev is the capital and largest city in Ukraine.

pride for Ukrainians eager to showcase their heritage, but for the most part the Kievans are far too busy struggling to survive to spend much time enjoying them.

KHARKOV, DNIPROPETROVSK, AND DONETSK

The three major cities of the eastern Ukraine are Kharkov, Dnipropetrovsk, and Donetsk. The city of Kharkov (Kharkiv in Ukrainian), in eastern Ukraine, is the country's second largest city, with 1.6 million inhabitants. According to travel writer Ryan Ver Berkmoes, Kharkov "is a surprisingly likable combination of old and new, narrow and spacious, gray and green, with numerous parks to stroll and a distinctive student feel to its lively streets."[3] Its proximity to the Russian border has, over

UKRAINIAN AND RUSSIAN SPELLINGS

Over centuries of domination by Russian speakers, Ukrainian cities started to be called by more Russian-sounding versions of their names. These names have become more familiar worldwide than their Ukrainian versions, and for this reason, Russian spellings will be used in this book. Over time, as the Ukrainian language becomes better established, the new spellings will become more widely known, including these versions of the following key places:

Russian Spelling	Ukrainian Spelling
Kiev	Kyiv
Chernobyl	Chornobyl
Lvov	Lviv
Kharkov	Kharkiv
Odessa	Odesa

In addition, Ukrainians feel that the designation "the Ukraine" implies a region within a larger nation, much as Americans refer to "the Midwest," for example. Thus, the name of the country is now properly "Ukraine" rather than "the Ukraine."

time, created strong cultural and ethnic ties to Russia, and in fact Kharkov, not Kiev, was the first capital of the Ukrainian Socialist Republic. A center of manufacturing and industry, Kharkov was heavily bombarded in World War II but has been rebuilt today into a center for the manufacture of tractors, engines, and other machinery.

Dnipropetrovsk, with a little over a million residents, is the third largest city in Ukraine. For decades a closed city, considered too valuable militarily to risk observation by outsiders, Dnipropetrovsk, named after the Dnieper River that runs through it, is still one of the major industrial strongholds of the nation. Dnipropetrovsk was founded in 1787 by the Cossacks, a fabled band of independent spirits and outlaws, but nothing remains today from that era.

Donetsk, like Dnipropetrovsk, is a working city that has had little time to beautify. The same size as Dnipropetrovsk, at a little over a million inhabitants, Donetsk is the heart of Ukraine's mining and industrial region and the capital of the Donbass region. Donetsk is close to the Russian border and, like Dnipropetrovsk, retains close cultural links to Russia. Donetsk and other surrounding cities and towns have fallen on hard times since the demise of the Soviet Union. The general dreary surroundings are aggravated by pollution and underemployment, and the crumbling mines kill and injure dozens of miners each year.

ODESSA

Approximately the same size as both Donetsk and Dnipropetrovsk, the city of Odessa (Odesa in Ukrainian) on the Black Sea coast could not be more different in all other respects. According to Ryan Ver Berkmoes, Odessa is "a potent brew of diverse ingredients yielding a strange southern magic. It is the country's biggest commercial Black Sea port, a hectic industrial city with polluted seas, and an enticing holiday center where people flock to laze on beaches and stroll through leafy streets."[4] Odessa's city center reveals its cultural mix, from a famous opera house in an ornate Baroque style to the five-domed blue and white Cathedral of the Assumption. The most famous landmark in Odessa is the Potemkin Steps. This long staircase, 192 steps in all, stretches from the city center, located on a bluff above the ocean, down to the harbor.

The ornate opera house is one of many famous landmarks in the Black Sea port city of Odessa.

LVOV

With approximately 800,000 residents, by far the smallest of the major cities of Ukraine, Lvov (Lviv in Ukrainian) nevertheless is one of the most important. Lvov is different from other major Ukrainian cities in that it, along with the rest of western Ukraine and Transcarpathia, was part of Poland until World War II. Thus it looks more like other cities in Central Europe, its skyline a mix of towers and church spires rather than the characteristic onion domes of Russia. Lvov is also a busy commercial and industrial city and has, according to Ver Berkmoes, "its share of decrepit communist-era industry and housing estates on the outskirts."[5] Yet Lvov is best known for its historic old town, which centers on Ploshcha Rynok, the best preserved old market square in Ukraine.

THE CULTURAL MAP OF UKRAINE

The city of Lvov serves as an illustration of the fact that Ukraine is divided not just into geographically distinct sections but into cultural regions as well. Though people of the country tend to live in regions that look similar, this does not necessarily mean that they feel they have much in common. Thus, to understand the modern nation of Ukraine, it is important to look at the map of the country another way, taking into account its history and patterns of settlement.

The huge, open stretches of steppe have left the region vulnerable to invasion by outsiders for several millennia. In the last two centuries, the borders of Ukraine have continually shifted as neighboring powers battled with each other to expand their empires. The two bordering countries having the greatest impact on today's Ukraine are Poland and Russia. Poland is a thoroughly European country. Its primary trade links over the centuries have been with other European cities, and it shares the Roman Catholic religion with much of Europe. Its artists, writers, and composers have followed Western traditions and artistic movements, so its culture is similar to those found elsewhere in Europe.

Russia, on the other hand, has a more mixed relationship with the West. It is so huge that it borders not only Europe but also China, and it crosses eleven of the world's twenty-four time zones. Although for several centuries Russia worked hard to establish trade and cultural links to Europe, it is too complex

THE POTEMKIN STEPS

Odessa is an intriguing city, renowned for its mix of architectural styles. Beautiful and classic Russian onion-domed churches and ornately decorated public buildings share neighborhoods with quickly constructed and now ugly and shabby Soviet era buildings. This mixture makes it similar to many other Ukrainian cities, but Odessa has one landmark by which it can be immediately identified. That landmark is the Potemkin Steps.

Grigory Potemkin was the one-eyed lover of eighteenth-century Russian empress Catherine the Great. Responsible for orchestrating Catherine's famed tour of the southern reaches of her empire, Potemkin had fake villages built along the route, literally no more than false fronts such as those now found on movie lots, in order to be sure Catherine would be pleased with what she saw. Many have commented on the similarity between Potemkin's efforts to disguise reality and those of the Communists two centuries later, giving rise to the derogatory term *pokazuhka*, meaning "only for show."

Potemkin's efforts to promote the development of port cities on the Black Sea were effective, and he is an important historical figure in the region. For this reason the staircase connecting the Odessa harbor with the city is named for him. The steps became an internationally known landmark as a result of a 1925 movie, *Battleship Potemkin*, by renowned Russian silent-film director Sergei Eisenstein. The epic film tells the true story of a mutiny on the battleship Potemkin set off by maggot-laden food rations. The most famous scene is of citizens of Odessa running down the steps to show support for the sailors. When the tsar's troops fire on them, bodies fall down the steps. Eisenstein enhanced the nightmarish quality of this scene by an innovative technique of switching shots every few seconds. At the opposite extreme, he stretched out one unforgettable image to its full length—a baby carriage, with baby still inside, bouncing down all 192 steps. Many directors since have praised—and copied—Eisenstein's ability to create heart-stopping suspense and horror by such techniques.

The Potemkin Steps became a famous landmark because of the 1925 movie Battleship Potemkin.

THE CHURCHES OF UKRAINE

Although practice of all religions was heavily discouraged and often punished during the Soviet era, religious faith never died in Ukraine. In the first years after independence, the three main Christian churches in Ukraine experienced revivals and now play an important role in the political as well as religious life of the nation.

The first, the Ukrainian Orthodox Church, is fundamentally a branch of the Russian Orthodox Church, having the Moscow patriarch as its spiritual head. Services follow the same pattern as the Russian Orthodox Church but are conducted in Ukrainian.

The second is the Ukrainian Autocephalous Orthodox Church. Its practices are essentially the same as the Ukrainian Orthodox Church, but its head is independent (the meaning of the word *autocephalous*); its patriarch, or spiritual head, is housed in Kiev. During the 1930s, when Soviet dictator Joseph Stalin was trying to break Ukrainians' ethnic identification and force them to think of themselves only as Soviet citizens, the Ukrainian Autocephalous Orthodox Church was outlawed. It was revived only in 1990, during the final year of the Soviet Union, in large part as a way of sending the message that Ukrainians intended to be masters of their own lives, free to worship as they wished. Recently the Ukrainian Autocephalous Orthodox Church divided into two branches, one calling itself by the same name and the other calling itself, somewhat confusingly, the Ukrainian Orthodox Church-Kiev Patriarchate to distinguish itself from the Moscow-centered Orthodox Church.

The third church is the Uniate, or Ukrainian Catholic Church. Founded in 1596, it essentially follows Orthodox rituals and traditions but maintains Catholic beliefs. For example, it recognizes the pope as its spiritual head, but differs from all other Catholics in that its priests are permitted to marry. This church is primarily found in right-bank, or western, Ukraine, where it evolved as a way of compromise between the Catholic Poles and the Orthodox Ukrainians. Stalin also outlawed the Uniate Church, and confiscated all its property, turning much of it over to the Russian Orthodox Church. The Uniate Church remained underground until the Ukrainian independence movement gathered steam in the 1980s.

Religious disunity is seen by some as a problem, symptomatic of the conflicts and divisiveness permeating all aspects of Ukrainian society. Others see the willingness to tolerate several churches as a good sign, perhaps signaling that the country will find ways to embrace a diversity of viewpoints on other matters.

ethnically and historically to be at heart a European country. Its religion is a form of Orthodox Christianity, having its roots in the Byzantine Church, centered in the Middle East. It uses its own alphabet, Cyrillic, a variant on the ancient Greek alphabet, also a sign of its non-European origins. Its music, art, and much of its overall culture is rooted in the region known as Central Asia.

These conflicting orientations have had a great effect on Ukraine. Despite the fact that ethnic Poles, Ukrainians, and Russians all are what are known as Eastern Slavs, and have strong ethnic links going back for centuries, they have evolved into distinct cultures with an uneasy relationship with each other. It is not clear among Ukrainians whether they are a European people looking westward for their natural linkages or a Central Asian one still looking primarily toward Russia for their strongest natural alliance.

LEFT BANK AND RIGHT BANK UKRAINE

The geographical landmark most clearly associated with this division of thought is the Dnieper River (Dnipro in Ukrainian).

The Dnieper River runs from north to south and divides Ukraine in half.

The Dnieper River runs from north to south and divides today's Ukraine neatly in half. It has served as the historical dividing line between those who looked westward toward Poland and the rest of Europe and those who looked east and northward toward Russia. For many years, it also served as the actual border between those two countries. Russia's control of the region is illustrated by the designation of the left and right banks of the Dnieper. The orientation is not that of a world map but the way the region would appear looking south from the vantage point of Moscow. In other words, the left bank is the eastern portion rather than the western, as one might presume from consulting a standard map with north at the top. On the right bank, or western Ukraine, a great deal more cultural diversity evolved. Whereas left bank residents came to consider themselves a part of Russia rather than a separate territory under Russian control, right bank residents were generally either Poles who had moved into what they were told was simply a new part of Poland or ethnic Ukrainians with long historical ties to the region.

Poland's control over western Ukraine came and went over the years, ending after World War II, and as a result a great deal of cultural intermixing had occurred and the culture of western Ukraine had taken on distinctly European elements. One of the most noticeable blended elements was the Uniate, or Ukrainian Catholic Church, sanctioned by the Roman Catholic Church as a means to avoid losing Ukrainian Christians to the Orthodox faith. The Uniate was a hybrid of Eastern Orthodoxy and Roman Catholicism, keeping many of the Orthodox practices but recognizing the pope as its spiritual head. This union was achieved only by the Catholic Church's willingness to continue to allow those elements of Orthodox faith compatible with Catholicism to remain intact, rather than requiring, for example, substitution of the Catholic mass and Catholic holidays for Orthodox ones.

Though Ukraine still saw itself as a region rather than as a nation, the concept of a legitimate Ukrainian nation began to evolve in western Ukraine in 1795, when Russia took control of the region from Poland. Domination by a foreign power that considered itself superior began to bother many western Ukrainians, as well as the Poles who had resettled there. In eastern Ukraine, however, no such nationalist stirrings occurred. There, ethnic Ukrainians were generally trying to minimize the differences between themselves and ethnic Russians, because power and prestige went with being Russian. Clearly by this point, being from Ukraine already meant very different things to different people.

THE LEGACY OF DIVISION

Today, this east-west conflict of attitudes is still clear. Not surprisingly, in the final days of the Soviet Empire, Lvov, in western Ukraine, became the center of efforts to declare independence. In western Ukraine today the language of choice is Ukrainian, and those who choose to address a local person in Russian are often perceived as insensitive, despite the fact that nearly all Ukrainians are fluent in that language—sometimes far better than in their own. East of the Dnieper River, the situation is reversed. Many citizens of

PYSANKY

Ukrainians are renowned for the beautiful designs with which they decorate their native costumes and other objects. The most famous Ukrainian decorative tradition is *pysanky*. *Pysanky* are hollowed-out eggs painted with elaborate designs. Although they have come to be associated with Easter, in fact the tradition of decorating eggs predates the Christian era in Ukraine. Authentic *pysanky* are made using an elaborate heated wax process, but a new variety made from wooden eggs has now evolved as a less fragile alternative for people who wish to purchase them as souvenirs.

There are hundreds of traditional *pysanky* patterns, varying from village to village. Each pattern has special symbolic meaning, and in the words of author Meredith Dalton, in *Culture Shock: Ukraine*, the designs are "truly fantastic."

Each pattern on a pysanky *has a special symbolic meaning.*

today's Ukraine, especially those in the east, barely know Ukrainian at all.

Though eastern Ukrainians voted overwhelmingly for independence, their decision was primarily an economic and political one, not in any way an attempt to break close ties with Russia. These ties run far deeper than simply language. The Orthodox faith links them more closely to Russia than to the Ukrainian Catholic faith of many western Ukrainians, and their culture is in many other respects fully blended with Russia's. Known as Russified Ukrainians, those east of the Dnieper have steadfastly opposed what they perceive as western desires to throw out centuries of history in order to create a separate Ukrainian identity, one they feel is falsely linked more closely to Europe than to Russia and the rest of Central Asia.

CRIMEA

Perhaps the best illustration of the challenges modern Ukraine faces in establishing a national identity can be found in

Crimea. This peninsula was made part of Ukraine by former premier Nikita Khrushchev in a gesture meant only to be symbolic, for the entire region was part of the Soviet Union anyway. However, when Ukraine declared independence, all of its territory went with it. Crimea is the only part of Ukraine that has no strong ethnic ties to the rest of the country. Even the most Russified people of eastern Ukraine still consider themselves to be from Ukraine rather than from Russia. Intermarriage over several centuries has also created at least some mixing of ethnic stock between Ukrainians and Russians, making it difficult for anyone to deny, even if they wished to, that they are not, at least in some sense of the word, "Ukrainian."

Crimea, in contrast, is not Ukrainian by any meaningful definition of the word. In this isolated near-island to the south, ethnic stock is Russian and Tatar, going back to the Mongol invasions of centuries before. Though the Tatars were exiled during Stalin's frequent rages against non-Russian people, Crimea is still the ancestral home for many of them. Most of the rest of the residents of Crimea are Russians, largely unmixed culturally or by marriage with Ukrainians. Though they voted for

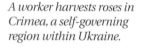

A worker harvests roses in Crimea, a self-governing region within Ukraine.

Ukraine's independence in 1991, only a small majority (54 percent) favored it, compared to figures above 80 percent even in the eastern Ukraine and above 90 percent in the west. Today Crimea has special status as a self-governing region within Ukraine, but its ultimate political destiny is unclear.

BEING UKRAINIAN

Just as the wooded steppe gives way by degrees, rather than suddenly, to the black soil of the south, there is no clear marker of what makes a person Ukrainian or not Ukrainian. The last census illustrates how difficult an issue this is. There are, at one extreme, Ukrainian citizens who identify as ethnic Ukrainian and speak Ukrainian and, on the other, citizens of Ukraine who are not ethnic Ukrainians and who speak only Russian. Many types of Ukrainians fall in between these extremes. To ask a person if he or she is Ukrainian is to invite a tangled web of questions about what in fact that means. Though all may look at a photograph of the wheat fields of the south, or the wooded plains of the center, and say "that is my homeland," they might agree on little else about what that homeland is or should become. This, to many, is the issue on which the future of Ukraine hinges.

2

FROM CONQUERORS TO CONQUERED

When the ancient Scythians of Central Asia swept on horseback onto the plains north of the Black Sea in the seventh century B.C., they must have felt they had found an earthly paradise. Many others have since shared their view; over the centuries, Ukraine has been coveted by many and conquered in turn by one group after another. Usually the people settling in Ukraine have managed to get along and eventually create a blended culture with those who already lived there. Nevertheless, Ukraine's history has many elements that are the complete opposite of paradise. Neighboring rulers' extremely violent and often devious attempts to add to their own territory have led to cruel subjugation of the people of this fertile and strategic land. With it came the imposition of outsiders' values and customs, without any concern for those who already lived there. Even today, while Ukraine is enriched by this diversity, it is also harmed by the lack of stability and weak national identity that are the legacy of centuries of outside rule.

EARLY SETTLERS

Relatively temperate weather in the south, rich soil, and easy travel on land and by river attracted Scythians in large numbers between the seventh and fourth centuries B.C., though there is evidence that early humans lived in the region from Paleolithic times, Scythian is the first culture about which much of anything is known. Roughly in the same era, ancient Greeks also arrived by boat on the shores of the Black Sea and set up colonies there. They traded with the Scythians, and though they often got into battles with each other they also got along well enough to intermarry and create a rich combined culture in the area of today's Ukraine. In fact, the Scythians' reputation as the finest gold workers of their era is actually known to be a result of Greek technology and teaching.

KIEVAN RUS

A series of other early groups came and went over the next few centuries, but the first group to have a role in today's Ukraine were the Slavs, from today's Poland, who by the sixth century A.D. had spread over much of Ukraine. From that point on, the lands of Ukraine were primarily populated by an ethnic group known collectively as the Eastern Slavs. Over time these Eastern Slavs would take on more specific identities as Ukrainians, Belarusans, and Russians.

The Scythians were some of the earliest settlers of the area now known as Ukraine.

Because the early groups before the Slavs left little in the way of a cultural or political legacy, when discussing the history of Ukraine, most historians consider it to have begun around the sixth century, with the rise of a powerful empire around Kiev, which became known as Kievan Rus. Kiev was not actually founded by Slavs but by the Varyagians, the name by which the Vikings (originally from Scandinavia) were locally known. By the end of the fifth century, the Varyagians, who had originally come down the Dnieper River to trade, had settled permanently along their trade routes. However, though the city may have Viking origins, according to writer Meredith Dalton, "there is consensus that the Scandinavian impact on Eastern Slavic language and culture was minimal,"[6] and the Scandinavians became assimilated into Slavic culture rather than the other way around.

CONVERSION TO CHRISTIANITY

Though the city of Kiev, with its rich ethnic mix, was a bustling trading center by the end of the ninth century, it did not exert any strong control over the surrounding communities. However, under prince Oleh the Wise in the years

THE CONTROVERSY OVER KIEVAN RUS

Although it is clear that Kievan Rus was the center from which Ukrainian, Belarusan, and Russian cultures evolved, the issue dividing some historians is whether the culture established in Kievan Rus simply moved eastward to Moscow or if Moscow created a new culture of its own. Though to outsiders this might seem unimportant, it has been an essential element in relations between Ukraine and Russia over the centuries. According to renowned historian Anatol Lieven, writing in *Ukraine and Russia: Fraternal Rivalry*, "many nationalists on both sides . . . are literally obsessed by this issue."

Some Russian historians argue that if the center of Kievan Rus culture simply shifted to Moscow, then Ukraine and Russia share a common culture and Moscow is now the legitimate center of that culture. This position was favored by both the tsars and the Communist leadership, who called "Kievan Rus" by the name "Old Rus." Other historians claim that Kievan Rus stayed centered in Kiev and the Muscovites branched off and established a separate although similar culture.

The controversy is an old one. Russian tsars insisted that they were the legitimate rulers of all the regions covered by the term *Rus*, which included Belarus as well as Ukraine and Russia, and thus were entitled to keep their lands together by force if necessary. Later, after the Russian Revolution deposed the tsars, Communist leaders took the same position and surpassed the tsars in the brutality of their suppression of Ukrainian autonomy. Today many Russians (including some ethnic Russians living in Ukraine) still do not accept that Ukraine is legitimately an independent country.

Most historians outside Ukraine and Russia (and many within as well) feel that because so much time has passed since Kievan Rus was at its peak, such historical debates make little sense. This controversy illustrates, however, how difficult it is to write history objectively. Though it is based on facts about the past, these facts are selected and interpreted by people living now, and are often colored by their own wishes, hopes, and needs.

around 900 A.D., the surrounding regions were brought together into one kingdom, ruled by a dynasty known as the Princes of Kiev. Approximately a century later, under Prince Volodymyr, the region now known as Kievan Rus had become a significant regional power. Its power was limited and precarious though, as it was caught between several other great empires on its borders. At the time, these other empires were distinguished by their practice of different religions. To the east of Kievan Rus, Orthodox Christianity dominated, whereas in the west, the Holy Roman Empire practiced Roman Catholicism. To the south, Islam was growing in strength in the eastern Mediterranean.

Volodymyr sensed that his kingdom would have to choose an alliance with one of these powers or be swallowed up by one or all three of them. The key to this alliance was conversion, and in the end Volodymyr chose the Orthodox Christianity of the Byzantine Empire, not out of any profound religious sentiments but as a political strategy. Volodymyr held mass baptisms by driving the people of Kiev into the freezing Dnieper River, which from that point forward marked the western boundary of what became known as Orthodox Christianity. Because religion is one of the things that brings people together or tears them apart, Volodymyr's conversion set in motion friendships and enmities between western and eastern Ukrainian Christians that have shaped history into the present era.

THE GLORY DAYS AND DECLINE OF KIEVAN RUS

According to historian Daniel C. Diller, under Volodymyr's successors, Kievan culture "reached its zenith with great advances made in the areas of law, art and architecture, and education."[7] Volodymyr's son Yaroslav the Wise established the

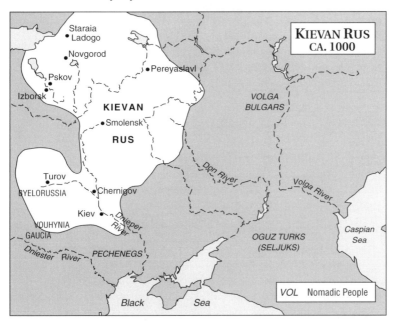

first schools, library, and written codes of law. Yaroslav is also known by the nickname "Father-in-law of Europe," because of his success in marrying his sons and daughters to royalty in countries such as Poland, Hungary, Norway, and France. Yaroslav actually ruled only the part of Kievan Rus west of the Dnieper River; his brother Mstyslav ruled the eastern portion.

Yaroslav's part of Kievan Rus was as advanced as any culture of the time in Europe, and in fact, the emissary sent by King Henri I of France to ask (successfully) for Yaroslav's daughter Anna's hand in marriage reported back that "this land is more unified, happier, stronger, and more civilized

THE CONVERSION OF VOLODYMYR

The earliest written Rus history, the *Chronicle of Bygone Years*, quoted in Anna Reid's *Borderland*, contains an account of Volodymyr's search for a religion. As a young man Volodymyr worshiped pagan gods, setting up statues as objects of worship and human sacrifice all over his lands. He was also an enthusiastic womanizer. The *Chronicle* reports that he was "overcome with lust" and "insatiable with vice," maintaining hundreds of women as concubines in his various palaces. Volodymyr knew he needed to find a religion to strengthen his political alliance with one of his neighbors, but he was looking for one that would not demand that he change his lifestyle too much.

He first looked into the possibility of converting to Islam, consulting with the Muslim Bulgars. "Volodymyr listened to them, for he was fond of women and indulgence.... But circumcision and abstinence from pork and wine were disagreeable to him: 'Drinking,' said he, 'is the joy of the Russes, and we cannot exist without that pleasure.'" He then sent emissaries to Catholic cities in today's Germany, who reported back that they "saw them performing many ceremonies in their temples," but "beheld no glory there." But when his emissaries went to the Hagia Sophia, a huge and historic church in today's Istanbul, they were astonished. "We knew not whether we were in heaven or on earth. For on earth there is no such splendor or beauty, and we are at a loss how to describe it. We only know that God dwells there among men, and their service is fairer than the ceremonies of other nations."

Volodymyr was dazzled by these descriptions, and because it seemed he could become an Orthodox Christian without giving up his lifestyle, he was soon baptized. This ceremony would prove to be, in the words of Anna Reid, "one of the single most important events in the history of Europe."

than France herself."[8] Literacy was also more advanced in Kievan Rus than in France. This is evidenced by surviving documents that show only crosses for French signatures, but the name "Anna Regina," or Queen Anna, written out clearly on those from Kievan Rus.

Yaroslav indeed lived up to his name "the Wise," having a keen sense of how to create alliances with foreigners and build a sense of pride in his own subjects. But in 1054, when Yaroslav was dying, he made a strategic error that set in motion the decline of Kievan Rus. Instead of offering his kingdom to one of his five sons, he divided Kievan Rus into separate princedoms, and soon each prince was at war with the others. During this era, known as the Appanage period, the people of Kievan Rus began to move away, probably in response to the tensions created by the warring princes. These migrations set in motion the division of the eastern Slavic people into Belarusans, Russians, and Ukrainians. Most significant of these migrants was the group that wandered northeast and established the empire then known as Muscovy, which later became the heart of Russian culture and power. The immediate effect on Kievan Rus, however, was a loss of population just as a powerful threat was growing in the east.

By the early thirteenth century, Kievan Rus fell to one of the great invading powers of the era, the Mongols, known in Eastern Europe as Tatars. The Mongols originated in northwestern China, and by the time they reached Kievan Rus in 1240 they had already conquered southern Siberia, Central Asia, and Iran. Kiev, including its nearly four hundred churches, was burned to the ground by Mongol leader Batuy's army, and its protective earthen walls, or ramparts, were leveled. Kiev never recovered. Because the Mongols favored Moscow as their regional capital, they abandoned Kiev after only two years. From then on, the region once glorified as Kievan Rus took on the name Ukraina, or "borderland." Kiev was soon also relieved of its status as home to the metropolitan, the highest ranking Orthodox church leader. He moved to the town of Vladimir, near Moscow, and then after a few decades to Moscow itself. For five hundred years after the attack by the Mongols, Kiev remained a provincial outpost, barely a city at all. Russian empress Catherine the Great passed through on her way to Crimea in 1787 and wrote, "I

have looked around for a city, but so far I have found only
two fortresses and some outlying settlements."[9]

THE GALICIAN-VOLHYNIAN PRINCIPALITY

Though Ukraine was seen as a borderland of no particular interest to Moscow, it remained a source of much political ma-
neuvering. For a while, one of the warring princes, Roman
Mstyslavych, was able to establish control over the western
Galician and Volhyn regions, which today constitute most of
Ukraine's west, south, and center. He established the Galician-
Volhynian Principality in 1203, but it lasted only a few generations. Nevertheless, it was one of the few times since the fall
of Kievan Rus that Ukraine was not ruled by outsiders.

The principality was short-lived and eventually fell under
the control of the combined kingdom of Poland and Lithuania. From the late fourteenth century until the mid seven-
teenth, most of the region encompassed by today's Ukraine
was considered to be part of Poland. This turn of events was
also momentous for future history, because it set up a divisiveness between western parts of Ukraine, which adopted
much of Polish culture, and the east, which remained
strongly Orthodox, and in some parts Muslim.

THE COSSACKS

No one, on the other hand, was able to exert much influence
or control over the steppe region to the south and east. This
region became in many respects the equivalent of the American "Wild West," home to highly individualistic adventurers
and outcasts from other cultures. According to writer Ryan
Ver Berkmoes, by the late fifteenth century "the area attracted runaway serfs, criminals, Orthodox refugees, and
other misfits from Polish and Lithuanian domains to the
north-west."[10] They began to be known as *kazaks* (or Cossacks in English), from a Turkish word with several mean-
ings, including outlaw, free person, and adventurer.

The best known group of Ukrainian Cossacks were the Zaporizky, who founded an island fortress community known
as Zaporizky Sich. Cossack communities such as Zaporizky
Sich were independent of each other, ruled by elected leaders called *hetmans*, who presided over the *rada*, an open air
gathering where loud and often drunken discussions among
all the men of the community were held. Most of the time the

vast majority of Cossacks stayed home and farmed and raised families, but according to Anna Reid, "when the inclination and the hetman dictated, they took up horsetail banners and spiked maces, and launched fearsome raids deep into Poland,"[11] as well as into Russia, Turkey, and other neighboring regions. It was their victory against the Poles in a Ukrainian revolt in 1648, led by Bohdan Khmelnytsky, that made it clear once and for all that they would be a force to be reckoned with by anyone who wanted to control Ukraine. Ironically, however, it was also Khmelnytsky who set in motion the downfall of the Cossacks when he formed a disastrous alliance with Russia.

CREATING A HERO

According to Meredith Dalton in *Culture Shock: Ukraine*, "that [Bohdan] Khmelnytsky is regarded as a hero by many is a source of great tension in Ukraine." Although he stood up to the Poles and undoubtedly in that way gave Ukrainians a powerful symbol of their ability to fight back against their enemies, his legacy is tainted by his extreme anti-Semitism and by his willingness to ally with Russia.

Nearly a quarter-million Jews, most simple farmers or merchants and their families, were killed for no reason other than prejudice and bloodlust during the period when Khmelnytsky's bands of Cossacks roamed the countryside. Ukrainians of Polish origin also suffered greatly under the Cossacks and do not see them or Khmelnytsky as anything to revere.

The other criticism of Khmelnytsky, that he betrayed Ukraine to the Russians, is less clearly justifiable. Obviously at the time, Khmelnytsky could not have known what his actions would unleash, and he was right that Cossack-dominated Ukraine needed a strong ally. Still, many today wonder why a man whose greatest historical contribution ended up causing so much harm is being touted as a hero.

Anna Reid explains in *Borderland* that "the Ukrainian version of events, of course, is that Khmelnytsky led an early, failed war of independence," and for that he deserves his status as national hero. However, there is no evidence that he had such grand motives; documents from the era show that his interests scarcely went beyond improving the position of the Cossacks themselves, not the general population. But, as Reid explains, Ukrainians are working to create a separate, national history at this point, and "for a country short on heroes, he is simply too prominent to pass up."

PARTITIONS OF POLAND

To RUSSIA

To PRUSSIA

To AUSTRIA

First Partition (1772)
Second Partition (1793)
Third Partition (1795)

Russia was by the mid-1600s a huge empire, although not as powerful as it wanted to be. It was very isolated, having no strong trade links to Europe, and only lightly populated in most areas. Khmelnytsky thought an alliance with Russia would keep outsiders such as the Poles at bay, but from the beginning it was clear this was not to be an alliance of equals. Barely after the ink was dry, a new era known as "the Deluge" by Poles and "the Ruin" by Ukrainians began. Russian, Polish, Tatar, and Cossack armies fought for supremacy everywhere in the Ukraine, raping, pillaging, murdering, and destroying crops and buildings as they went. The end of this period came in 1667 with the Treaty of Andrusovo, optimistically but inaccurately called an "eternal peace." Poland and Russia agreed that from then on Kiev and all lands east of the Dnieper would belong to Russia, and the lands west would belong to Poland. The Cossacks were not even invited to attend the treaty discussions. Ukraine had simply been divided and given away.

RUSSIFICATION

By the mid–eighteenth century, Poland was deeply divided by internal conflicts and was, in the words of Frederick of Prussia, "like an artichoke, ready to be eaten leaf by leaf."[12] In 1773 and again in 1793, the surrounding powers of Russia, Prussia, and Austria divided up Poland among themselves, with Poland helpless to keep it from happening. Finally, in the last partition, in 1795, Poland ceased to exist altogether. This had an immediate impact on Ukraine, because west of the Dnieper was Polish territory. When Poland was wiped from the map, its portion of Ukraine went with it. All Ukraine was now part of the Russian Empire.

Almost immediately, the tsars made a concentrated effort to convince the people of Ukraine and Russia that Ukraine had always legitimately been Russian. Using Kievan Rus as a legendary starting point, Russian empress Catherine II claimed she was "gathering the Russian lands," and had a commemorative medal struck that said "I have recovered what was torn away."[13]

Russian empress Catherine II believed that Ukraine had always legitimately belonged to Russia.

Catherine's first step to undercut Ukrainian identity in what was subsequently referred to as "Little Russia" or "New Russia" was to make Cossack leaders Russian nobles. As such, they had special privileges such as tax exemptions and ownership of the lands they controlled. It became so advantageous socially and economically to be perceived as Russian that many Ukrainians, Cossack or otherwise, participated willingly in "Russification," changing the spellings of their names and teaching their children Russian rather than Ukrainian customs and language.

Those who were not willing to give up their own customs and culture soon discovered how far the Russian tsars would go. In the nineteenth century, Ukrainians of Polish background were sent by the thousands into exile in Siberia as punishment for even the slightest resistance to Russification. Polish nobles often lost their noble status and were forced into serfdom. Both Ukrainian and Polish schools were closed if they were not teaching in Russian, and in only a few decades the literacy rate of Ukraine became one of the lowest in Europe. Churches such as the Uniate were forced to "reunify" with the Russian Orthodox Church, which in effect meant little more than having their property seized and their practices forbidden.

In 1876, Tsar Alexander II signed the Edict of Ems, which banned all publications and all public presentations in Ukrainian. All teaching was to be in Russian, and anyone defying the edict risked being sent into exile. However, even though Ukrainians might have conformed on the surface, among many a pride in their own Ukrainian identity was growing. Various political groups and individuals tried, from the 1840s on, to encourage resistance by engaging in forbidden activities from using the Ukrainian language to revolting outright against Russian rule. For the most part, though, Ukraine remained politically quiet, its citizenry having settled in to at least a superficial Russian identity. Meanwhile, all around them the world was shifting dramatically and uneasily. In the first twenty years of the new century, Ukraine would again find itself beset by wars and competing political ideas.

WORLD WAR I

When World War I was declared in 1914, Ukrainians found themselves serving on both sides of the conflict, some in the Austrian army, but most (3.5 million by war's end) in the Russian army. Whereas in most wars people are willing to fight for their own country, many Ukrainians felt that they didn't really have a country to fight for. In fact, many of them would have been more than happy to see the Russians lose badly enough to lose control of Ukraine after the war. All over Ukraine, loyalties were divided. Those who wanted complete independence saw that there might be a chance to achieve this amid all the chaos, while others felt they were fighting for Mother Russia, their true and only homeland.

By mid-1915, the western regions of Ukraine and all of Belarus had been occupied by the Austrian and German armies. The Russians pushed back in 1916 and again in 1917 to try to regain control of Lvov and the surrounding region,

but they were unable to do so. Ukraine was in chaos. The country was occupied by the Germans, who seemed by this point likely to lose the war in the end. The Allied forces—France, Britain, the United States, and Russia—were stronger overall, but Russia was in total disarray, no longer an effective part of the Allied war effort. Within Ukraine, soldiers and civilians alike were confused about which side to support, because the two most important powers to them at the moment, Germany and Russia, both seemed to be in deep trouble. Anna Reid explains, "Accused of collaboration by both sides, Ukrainian civilians suffered terribly throughout, being shot, deported or interned in thousands."[14] Though Ukraine was used to having its cities and towns turned into battlefields, this was the worst destruction the country had ever witnessed.

Revolutionaries travel through the streets of St. Petersburg, Russia, in 1917.

THE RUSSIAN REVOLUTION

The reason for Russia's disarray was the Russian Revolution. In the first part of 1917, Tsar Nicholas II of Russia abdicated his throne and was exiled to the Russian countryside with his family. Later that year, Lenin and his supporters, called Bolsheviks, took power in Russia. However, their radical ideas, known as communism—abolishing private ownership of property and forcing people to work on collective farms and factories for little more than food and shelter—were not popular at all. The Bolsheviks knew that keeping power for long in Russia and its outlying regions would have to be done by force. They reasoned that once their ideas had been implemented, people would see them as true visionaries and be glad for what they had done, but in the short run dissenters would have to be put down by whatever means necessary.

Lenin and his Bolsheviks faced another problem: The war with Germany was still raging. Lenin was interested in getting out of the war so that he could turn his attention to strengthening his political base in Russia. Thus, in 1918, he and the Germans signed the Treaty of Brest-Litovsk. Russia agreed in the treaty to hand over possession of Ukraine, the Baltics, Russian-occupied Poland, and portions of Belarus to Germany in exchange for Russia's withdrawal from the war. Germany wanted to go a little further to sever the political and historical connection between Russia and Ukraine; as part of the Brest-Litovsk negotiations, Germany persuaded Russia to agree to let Ukraine declare itself an independent nation.

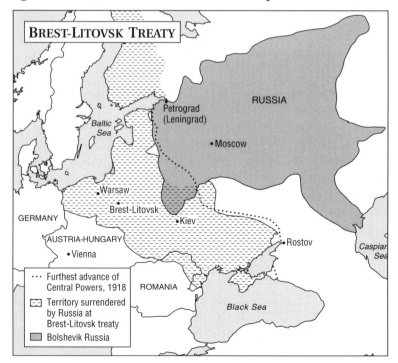

THE UKRAINIAN NATIONAL REPUBLIC

This independence was clearly only partial, because the Germans fully intended to move quickly to occupy Ukraine. Still, Ukrainians felt they were finally on the road to having their own country, free of Russian control. However, the new governing council for Ukraine, called by the old Cossack name Rada was doomed from the start by squabbles between its members. Few had any practical experience with politics or government, and most put political ideology and debate above the practical mat-

The signing of the Treaty of Brest-Litovsk allowed Ukraine to declare itself an independent nation.

ters of governing. Within a few months, in late 1917, pro-Bolshevik army units marched into Kiev, launching bombs across the Dnieper River into the center of the city. The Rada, recognizing that it could not hold on to power, issued a last declaration, this one announcing full independence for Ukraine. "People of Ukraine!" it said, "By your efforts, by your will, by your word, a Free Ukrainian People's Republic has been created on Ukrainian soil. The ancient dream of your ancestors . . . has been fulfilled."[15] Two weeks later the Rada fled Kiev by train, but all along their route to safety they continued to argue. In the words of a biographer of Mykhaylo Hrushevsky, the Rada president, "in various obscure towns along the railway line, laws were passed about the socialization of land . . . a new monetary system, a coat-of-arms for the Republic, Ukrainian citizenship,"[16] apparently without the Rada noticing that they no longer were really in charge of anything.

After the Treaty of Brest-Litovsk was signed, the Germans occupied Kiev, and Hrushevsky and the Rada were brought back to serve as the government again. Germany wanted to look as if it respected the political autonomy of Ukraine by permitting it to have its own people in charge. In fact, it intended to use the Rada as a "puppet government," a term used when an occupying power controls, or pulls the strings of, local government. However, as Reid writes, "a few weeks of the

Ukrainians' interminable bickering convinced them that the Rada was incapable of running even a puppet government."[17] Soldiers marched into the assembly and forcibly disbanded it, naming a wealthy local landowner "Hetman of All Ukraine." Peace reigned for the remainder of 1918, but the Germans were clearly losing the war. Later that year they withdrew from Kiev, and soon the war ended altogether, although the people of Ukraine were soon to find that this gave them little reason to rejoice.

PARTISAN WARFARE

Besides being a battle ground in a world war between 1914 and 1921, Ukraine was also the scene of a terrible civil war. In addition to hostilities between the Germans and the Allied forces, numerous other combatants were battling for control of Russia and its territories. The Bolsheviks, or Red Army, fought against both the Ukrainian nationalists, who wanted to break from Russia altogether, and the White Army, which wanted to restore the tsar and end Bolshevik rule but had little interest in or support for Ukrainian independence. Adding to the upheaval, many bands of outlaws, calling themselves Cossacks in order to give their sheer opportunism some semblance of glamour, pillaged the countryside. Altogether approximately 1.5 million people died as a result of the violence in Ukraine between 1914, the onset of World War I, and 1921, when the Bolsheviks finally triumphed. As in the past, Jews were especially victimized. At the hands of the White Army and Ukrainians in particular, they were robbed, raped, and killed, often with deliberate savagery.

The Allied forces were not content to let Ukraine fall into Communist hands, so they continued to do battle in the region as well. They and the Red, White, and Ukrainian forces took and lost control of varying patches of Ukrainian land with dizzying speed. Accounts vary as to whether Kiev changed hands twelve, fourteen, or eighteen times in the year and a half between the Treaty of Brest-Litovsk and the end of World War I, but even the smallest of these figures shows the extent of the chaos. At the end of World War I, one of the biggest concerns was the future of Ukraine. The Ukrainian nationalists did the best they could to gather support for full independence, but they were not successful. In the end, the United States cast the deciding vote against Ukrainian independence, giving away western Ukraine to Poland to strengthen that country as a buffer in the event of further Soviet military aggression. Partly out of ignorance, the United States and the other Allies went along with the Polish argument that there was no valid country of Ukraine, but mostly they did so out of fear that if they allowed Ukraine to stand on its own it would be quickly swallowed up by the Bolsheviks.

In the end, the Treaty of Versailles officially ended World War I, but far from giving Ukraine its independence, it split it instead into four sections, each controlled by a foreign government. Galicia and western Volhynia went to Poland. Central and eastern Ukraine went to Russia. Smaller regions bordering Romania and Czechoslovakia went to those countries. Warfare between Poland and the Soviet Union over their border was still being waged when the Treaty of Versailles was signed, so that particular border was left unclarified. As a sign of how totally disregarded the Ukrainians were in the wake of the Treaty of Versailles, when Poland and the Soviet Union negotiated the Treaty of Riga at the end of their separate war in 1921, no Ukrainian was even invited to participate in the discussion despite the fact that the border being drawn was on Ukrainian soil. This disrespect would be characteristic of the Soviet decades to come.

3

FROM SOVIET REPUBLIC TO INDEPENDENT NATION

Their country divided and in ruins, the eastern and central Ukrainians were exhausted and demoralized at the end of World War I. They were in no position to fight being absorbed into the Soviet Union when Lenin and the Bolsheviks soon became the undisputed rulers of the former Russian Empire. Their new status as the Ukrainian Socialist Republic seemed to many Ukrainians to be an improvement, though. Lenin appeared to favor allowing Ukraine and the other new socialist republics to retain their unique cultures, as long as they remained loyal to the Communist Party and to the Soviet Union. Lenin wanted the world to believe that communism had international appeal and was on the verge of spreading worldwide. He could do this best by presenting each new republic, including Ukraine, as culturally distinct but enthusiastically Communist.

As a result, according to Tim Smith in *Ukraine's Forbidden History,* "the 1920s were an extraordinarily rich period for the flowering of Ukrainian culture and a decisive phase in the creation of modern Ukraine."[18] Use of the Ukrainian language was encouraged, and historians and writers were also encouraged to pursue topics relating to Ukraine. However, this "flowering" was short lived, its decline initiated not by the government but by non-Ukrainians, particularly Russians and Jews living in the region. The Russians argued, as they had historically, that this new Ukrainian identity was false and that it stood in the way of establishing a strong Russian-dominated Soviet Union. The Jews were concerned because Ukrainian nationalists had in the past been among their worst persecutors. Soon Ukrainian nationalism was denounced by the government as well, and the period of "Ukrainianization" was over.

WESTERN UKRAINE AFTER WORLD WAR I

In Polish-controlled western Ukraine, there was not even a brief period of support for Ukrainian culture. Determined to create an extension of Poland in the region, the Polish government, especially after Polish nationalist Josef Pilsudski became president in a 1926 coup, launched a campaign equivalent to the Russification of previous centuries. Poland's goal, according to one of its top ministers, Stanislaw Grabkski, was "the transformation [of Ukraine] into Polish ethnic territory."[19] Ukrainian schools were closed if teachers refused to teach in Polish, Ukrainians were forbidden to hold even menial government jobs and were not permitted to run for office, and Ukrainian newspapers were severely censored.

Although the majority of Ukrainian politicians favored seeking compromise and cooperation, a strong underground movement grew, calling itself the Organization of Ukrainian Nationalists (OUN). The OUN favored violent tactics such as arson, beatings, and assassinations. Though its leaders were often caught and imprisoned, and the organization was bitterly divided by the 1930s into a moderate and a more radical wing, the OUN remained strong until World War II. At that point it formed the core of the Ukrainian Partisan Army, yet another group committed to achieving independence for their country.

Joseph Stalin chose Ukraine as the site of his first kolkhozes, or collective farms.

JOSEPH STALIN AND COLLECTIVIZATION

In eastern Ukraine, what seemed briefly to be a situation preferable to that in Poland quickly became far worse. In 1926 Lenin died of a stroke, and after a vicious struggle for power, Joseph Stalin emerged as the new leader of the Soviet Union. According to writer Ryan Ver Berkmoes, "when Stalin took power in 1927, he looked upon Ukraine as a laboratory for testing Soviet restructuring, while stamping out 'harmful' nationalism."[20] It was in Ukraine that Stalin chose to set up the first kolkhozes, or collective farms, and where he first unleashed his deadly efforts to force people to give up any identity other than that of loyal Soviet citizen.

Loyal Soviet citizens toil on one of Stalin's collective fish farms.

In 1929, Stalin began establishing kolkhozes in Ukraine. At first peasants were told that it would be in their best economic interests to be part of a collective, or large group of workers, rather than each family owning a small patch of land. They were encouraged to give up private ownership of their families' land in favor of working with neighbors to farm the huge fields created by pooling their resources. The Soviet government would own all the land (as well as manufacturing plants and other industries) on the people's behalf, collecting harvests and manufactured goods and redistributing them as needed across the country. The idea was that everyone would work hard, and in return have his or her basic needs met. The government claimed that this was the only way to end a society of rich and poor, exploited workers and overprivileged owners, and to have a fairer system put in its place.

Soon, however, it became apparent that those who did not volunteer to give up their land were viewed as enemies of the state. Peasants known as kulaks were particularly targeted. *Kulak* was the word used for what seems clearly to be a contradiction in terms: a "wealthy peasant." However, in Ukraine, as elsewhere in the Soviet Union, one might be

THE GULAG ARCHIPELAGO

The *Gulag Archipelago* is a term made famous by Alexander Solzhenitsyn, a Russian author who wrote a book by that name describing the network of prison camps established by Joseph Stalin and continuing on a smaller scale until the fall of the Soviet Union. As the word *archipelago* suggests, these camps, or gulags, were like innumerable islands, but rather than being surrounded by sea, they were mostly located in isolated and often nearly uninhabitable regions of the country. To these camps were sent hundreds of thousands of Soviet citizens, including many thousands of Ukrainians, sometimes for crimes such as murder or treason but often for no clear offense at all.

People sentenced to the gulags often were marched hundreds of miles on foot, or crammed so tightly into cattle cars on trains that those who died often could not fall to the floor. Food and water were woefully inadequate or not provided at all. In such conditions, human beings were moved, sometimes thousands of miles and often with their entire families, to camps that operated with similar disregard for their survival. In fact, their life or death was of no real importance. They were, after all, people the Soviet government considered poison, people they preferred dead but thought they might get some final use from.

Camps were generally located near some resource such as timber or a valuable metal to be mined. Prisoners were often worked until they collapsed and died, or until some excuse could be found to shoot them. The calories in their daily diets were far below what was required to maintain their bodies, and therefore the most common causes of death were slow starvation and disease caused by reduced physical health. However, new prisoners continually arrived, so deaths of existing ones were not considered a problem.

This account by a Ukrainian gulag survivor, quoted in Tim Smith's *Ukraine's Forbidden History*, is typical of what happened to those sentenced to the camps: "I was arrested and accused of saying things about Stalin. [I was] sent to Siberia to a camp, working in the forest cutting wood for fifteen hours a day. It was forty-five degrees below zero. It was just forest and nothing else. People were just dying because there were no buildings; we had to build everything." Though exact figures will never be known, millions died in the gulags.

branded wealthy for having two cows instead of one, or a sturdier roof than the ones on neighboring huts. Signs appeared in villages bearing slogans such as "those who do not join the kolkhoz are enemies of Soviet power. The heroic period of our socialist construction has arrived. The kulaks must be liquidated."[21]

In this "dekulakization" campaign, Stalin gave quotas to local Communist leaders, detailing exactly how many kulaks they needed to deport or execute in a given period of time. It didn't really matter who was shot or exiled as long as the quota was met. No one was safe. People were encouraged to tell on their neighbors, going to the police with reports that a family was hoarding candles or that an individual had not turned over all his potatoes to the community. Everything was to be turned over to the state. Nothing was to be privately owned, kept, or used without permission, and little acts, often born of desperation and hunger, became the equivalent of high treason. People were shot or deported for insignificant acts such as keeping an apple from a tree in their yard or putting a kernel of wheat in their mouth while laboring in the fields.

THE GREAT HUNGER

Stalin's Ukrainian "laboratory" took on even more deadly dimensions in the early 1930s. Dismayed by the low yields from the collective farms, Stalin's government began setting unrealistic goals for each harvest. All of the harvest up to the quota would be handed over to the state for storage in the event of emergency. What remained was available for the workers to eat. Thus, despite plentiful grain, livestock, and other food sources all around them, the Ukrainians were being systematically starved to death, because unrealistic goals meant there was never any surplus.

The Soviets denied the famine to the world, as whole villages slowly died. As peasants collapsed from starvation in the fields, Communist Party activists policed their labor, ready to shoot on sight if it appeared that anyone had stolen a morsel of food or had stopped working. Despite the fact that "there was food and plenty of it,"[22] this sustained policy of deliberate starvation is estimated to have killed between 5 and 7 million people in 1932 and 1933 alone. Though there was little hope of breaking free of the Soviet Union, after such a betrayal, Ukrainians lost what desire they may have felt to be part of the Communist empire. Memories of the deliberate starvation of the Ukrainians were still so vivid late in the century that when the Soviet Union appeared on the verge of collapse in the early 1990s, mention of the famines was enough to fan the flames of the independence movement.

THE GREAT TERROR

For Stalin, the famine was just a warm-up. Angered by the failure of collectivization in Ukraine, he blamed it on Ukrainians' lack of enthusiasm for communism. Stalin equated this lack of commitment with treason and unleashed a new campaign known as the Great Terror. Anyone could find him- or herself a target for death, prison, or deportation for any reason, however petty. No proof of disloyalty was required, and, as Tim Smith writes, "a form of collective madness swept Ukraine. This was a period when family members, friends, and neighbors disappeared overnight without explanation; when children informed on their parents for 'anti-revolutionary behavior'; when

The Soviet government's idea of a fair social system subjected Ukrainians to terror, famine, homelessness, and death.

Ukrainian writers and artists were arrested and subjected to show trials."[23]

People were selected, seemingly at random, for execution, often at night in the woods or secluded areas outside of towns. They were marched to a chosen spot and shot one by one, their bodies falling into pits, which were subsequently covered over when they were full. Such pits and other mass graves are still being uncovered in Ukraine today, largely as the efforts of volunteer groups such as Memorial that piece

 ## "LAUGHTER DISAPPEARED FROM THE VILLAGE"

Interviews collected by Tim Smith and the coauthors of *Ukraine's Forbidden History* describe the horrors of village life during the period of collectivization and famine.

In 1929 . . . party representatives visited every house and if the family refused to join the kolkhoz they were deprived of their property and sent to Siberia. They took our cow even though we were eleven children in our family— little ones—and my mother knelt down and begged. Some families were taken out of the village and thrown naked into the snow and they froze to death.

By 1931 everyone was in the kolkhoz. The starvation began in the autumn of 1931; absolutely everything was taken out of the village. They came to every house to search for bread. Laughter disappeared from the village. In spring 1932 people had to eat [wild] plants. We had to eat leaves from trees. 1933 was the worst; my whole family died. It was a terrible time, terrible.

Every house had dead people and two people from the kolkhoz had to bury them. They went to every house with a horse and cart and in the cemetery they made a common grave. They were taken like timber and every day there was a large harvest of dead people. Sometimes even people who were not dead but dying were taken and put in the grave. They thought it would save time.

My sister was asking my mother for something to eat, but there was no milk or bread. My sister wanted to eat her hands so my mother tied her hands to her side. People began to eat people, [cutting] off a hand, a piece of the body, in order not to die from hunger. In our village, 3000 people died, compared to 185 who died later in the war.

together information from survivors in order to locate graves and provide some means to honor the usually anonymous dead. It is still not clear how many Ukrainians died during the Great Terror, but conservative estimates place the number at well over a million, and it is probably much higher.

Those who were not executed were usually deported to work camps called gulags, often located in harsh arctic regions, where they were worked to death in mines or similar operations. Whole families were sometimes deported because of the perceived disloyalty of one member. Poorly clothed and starving, few survived a work camp sentence. In fact, many died before arrival during the forced marches without food, water, or medical attention. The goal, quite clearly, was not to have an effective workforce in the camps but to ensure that as many people as possible died in the process.

WORLD WAR II

The period between world wars lasted less than two decades. Joseph Stalin was still leader of the Soviet Union when, in 1939, he and Nazi Party leader, Adolf Hitler, by then chancellor of Germany, made a secret deal that would bring yet more suffering to Ukraine. The Molotov-Ribbentrop Pact, named after the two men who negotiated it, was an agreement between the Soviet Union and Germany not to go to war against each other, but instead to agree about a division of Poland. This was to be followed by a quick invasion to claim the agreed-upon territory. Both parties would in this way get land they craved without a loss of life or valuable military hardware. The invasion took place as planned, and western Ukraine became part of the Ukrainian Socialist Republic, establishing the western boundary still in place today.

Once the Soviet army had established control of western Ukraine, the process of what was now called "Sovietification" (as opposed to "Russification") began. Nikita Khrushchev, who would later replace Stalin as the leader of the Soviet Union, was by that point head of the Ukrainian Communist Party. He accepted his new responsibility for the expanded Ukraine with great enthusiasm, deporting Germans west across the border into Poland and forcing somewhere between 1 and 1.5 million western Ukrainians, primarily Poles and Jews, eastward into labor camps in Siberia and Kazakhstan.

Hitler broke the Molotov-Ribbentrop Pact with the Soviet Union by invading Ukraine in June 1941.

Germany did not abide by the Molotov-Ribbentrop nonaggression pact for long. In June 1941, Hitler's army invaded western Ukraine. Ironically, according to historian Daniel C. Diller, "the wave of terror during the Stalin era had made Soviet rule in Ukraine so unpopular that the German troops who invaded and occupied it in 1941 were cheered as saviors when they first arrived,"[24] and greeted with the traditional welcome of salt and bread. Ukrainian hopes of German support for an independent (but temporarily occupied) Ukraine, such as had been briefly achieved in World War I, were soon dashed when the Nazis began imprisoning and killing nationalist leaders.

Ukrainian Jews were treated with the same cold fury as Jews elsewhere in Europe. Special killing squads rounded up Jews in cities and villages. More than 100,000 Jews, one-third of the total population of Lvov, were killed or deported to camps, where most eventually died. In Odessa, almost 20,000 Jews were burned alive in one day. The single worst atrocity, one that has become symbolic of the Holocaust overall, was the massacre of almost 35,000 Jews at Babi Yar, in the northern region of Kiev. Evidence shows that Ukrainian police and many anti-Semitic citizens gladly played a role in the attempted extermination of the Jews, over 1 million of whom perished during the German occupation.

In 1942 another hardship hit the Ukraine. The German army needed more laborers for its mines, farms, and factories,

BABI YAR

In Ukraine, violent death and tremendous suffering have historically not been limited to any ethnic or social class, but undoubtedly Jews have suffered more than most.

When the German army invaded Ukraine in World War II, the mass extermination of Jews under way all over Europe extended eastward. Ukrainian Jews were soon rounded up by special units of the German army, the Einsatzgruppen. Many were deported or sent to death camps, but the easiest, and thus the usual, method of dealing with Jews was quick execution. The Jews of Kiev, for example, were rounded up in September 1941 and herded off to a wooded ravine called Babi Yar outside the city. Most went without a struggle, not just because there was little they could do against Nazi guns, but because they believed they were simply being organized for resettlement.

According to historian Anna Reid in *Borderland*, at Babi Yar, "the mouth of the ravine forms a precipice; men, women, and children were driven towards it in columns, and machine gunned by SS men [members of the Nazi Party] and Ukrainian militia from the opposite bank. The earth shoveled into the ravine when the operation was over did not cease moving for some time after," as those who were wounded or faked death were simply buried alive. Altogether, 33,771 Jews were killed in the two-day period of this one mass execution, although throughout the war, victims continued to be gunned down there. Babi Yar is only one of many killing grounds of World War II Ukraine and has become one of the most vivid symbols of Jewish suffering.

Babi Yar, the site of the two-day massacre of Kiev's Jews.

so it began forcibly relocating over a million young Ukrainians, mostly teenagers, to Germany. These workers, called "Ostarbeiters," or eastern workers, were in effect slaves, working long hours for the equivalent of pennies and suffering from malnutrition and medical neglect. Many young people chose to disappear to avoid what amounted to kidnapping, joining resistance movements such as the Ukrainian Insurgent Army (known as the UPA because of the initials of its Ukrainian spelling). Even after the war ended, the UPA remained in operation, fighting for an independent Ukraine against the Soviet forces that rolled in to retake control of the region. The organization was not finally suppressed until the 1950s.

YEARS OF SOVIET RULE

The period after World War II was one of relative quiet in Ukraine. Dissent was still dealt with quickly and usually fatally, especially until Stalin's death in 1953. Dissenters went deep underground, focusing on acts of military sabotage, and had little effect on the daily life of Ukrainians. Deportations to the gulags were still common—a half a million more Ukrainians ended up there in the 1950s alone. Russians occupied all positions of authority in Ukraine, and the Uniate Church, after having enjoyed a brief period of freedom, was once more forced into union with the Russian Orthodox Church.

When Nikita Khrushchev became the leader of the Soviet Union upon Stalin's death, he brought somewhat of a new style to Soviet government. Though unrealistic crop quotas were still set, Khrushchev did not approve of the murderous tactics that Stalin had used to enforce these quotas (although in earlier years, while building his own career, he had been one of these enforcers). Khrushchev and his successors tried a policy of greater freedom of expression in the arts and greater tolerance of regional cultures, but they easily became alarmed whenever this tolerance seemed disrespectful and injurious to the Soviet Union overall. Thus, the Khrushchev years from 1957 to 1964 and the years of Leonid Brezhnev from 1964 to 1982 were a time of wide swings in policy. They were also a period of general stagnation in the Soviet Union, including Ukraine.

DECLINE AND DECAY

In 1972, during the Brezhnev era in the Soviet Union, Volodymyr Shcherbytsky became the new Ukrainian Communist Party first secretary. He remained the highest ranking Communist official in Ukraine until 1989. Shcherbytsky was a close friend of Brezhnev from their early days in Dnipropetrovsk, when they were both rising stars in the Communist Party. Shcherbytsky fit the party's image of the ideal citizen, dubbed *homo sovieticus*, or "Soviet man." Soviet man felt no national or ethnic loyalty; rather, he considered himself only a loyal and committed citizen of the Communist state. Shcherbytsky was determined to make Ukraine a showcase for the success of communism.

The Soviet Union experienced a general period of stagnation under Prime Minister Nikita Krushchev.

He began his time in office by attacking any form of dissent, going so far as to "purge," or expel, half the members of the politburo, the ruling group of the party. He also purged thirty-seven thousand members of the party, justifying both moves on the grounds that those purged were not loyal or staunch enough supporters of communism. Many people expelled from the party were actually deeply committed to communism, but they were not true "Soviet men" because they also proudly saw themselves as Ukrainian. Those purged often found themselves deported to a gulag or imprisoned under harsh and even fatal conditions. By ridding Ukraine of anyone who hinted at having a sense of national pride, and by using the press, the schools, and the church as tools of indoctrination, Shcherbytsky was able to achieve the goal of creating a Soviet republic that at least on the surface seemed to be populated by dutiful, compliant "Soviet men."

THE GORBACHEV ERA

In 1985, while Shcherbytsky still controlled Ukraine, a new leader became head of the Soviet Union. Predicted initially to be a leader much like his predecessors, Mikhail Gorbachev quickly stunned not only the party but also the whole world by announcing the twin policies of glasnost and perestroika. Glasnost, or openness, meant that the government would make more efforts to speak honestly and frankly with the people and to be more tolerant of dissent. Perestroika, or restructuring, meant, among other things, that the Soviet Union would allow limited private ownership of property and businesses, and citizens would be able to participate in free elections.

Gorbachev was a committed Communist, but he was one of the few who understood that the Soviet Union was in deep economic trouble. Despite propaganda to the contrary, Communist workers were not even managing to feed themselves with their harvests, and their machinery and other manufactured goods were drastically inferior to those produced elsewhere. Gorbachev was convinced that communism would not last unless it was drastically reformed and that the key to those reforms was to get citizens to work harder and think more creatively. The best way to do this was to eliminate the threat of government reprisals if people spoke openly or

Soviet leader Mikhail Gorbachev took unprecedented steps to bring the Soviet Union out of its deep economic trouble.

acted independently, and to give people a chance to benefit directly and personally from their own labor.

Conservative Communists like Shcherbytsky were stunned by Gorbachev's ideas. They believed that a strong and even repressive government was needed to keep people from straying away from communist ideals. They thought if people could act independently of the government, making and spending money on their own and openly expressing ideas, they would lose respect for their leaders. Opponents of Gorbachev, including Shcherbytsky, reacted by continuing their oppressive tactics. Gorbachev was undeterred. Matters got worse for Shcherbytsky in 1987 when Gorbachev backed up his promises of reform by releasing thousands of political prisoners, including many Ukrainians imprisoned by the Ukrainian party secretary. Not only were the principles in which Shcherbytsky believed being undermined from the top, but the returning prisoners were taking advantage of glasnost to criticize Shcherbytsky's leadership openly and to lay the blame at his feet for their personal suffering in the gulags.

CHERNOBYL

Despite this new, open dissent, most Ukrainians continued to think it was best to avoid attracting the government's attention by testing whether it was serious about glasnost. Largely because of Shcherbytsky's effectiveness in promoting an environment of fear, Ukraine lagged behind many other Soviet republics such as Lithuania and Latvia that were using glasnost to clamor for independence. The Ukrainians' sentiments changed, however, when the world's worst nuclear accident happened near Kiev in April 1986.

At first, Gorbachev practiced the opposite of glasnost, denying that any problem had occurred, even when radiation detectors in Scandinavia and other parts of the world pinpointed the source of the massive radiation leaks as the nuclear reactors in the town of Chernobyl. In attempts to downplay the problem, no precautions were taken early on to minimize radiation exposure among either workers at the site or residents of the region. Shcherbytsky, who had been fully briefed on the seriousness of the radiation leak, ordered that May Day, the most important Soviet holiday, be celebrated as planned, while radioactive raindrops fell on paraders and picnickers all day. Only a handful of people died

WHAT HAPPENED AT CHERNOBYL?

The explosion at the nuclear power plant at Chernobyl, north of Kiev, near the border with Belarus, was the result of an ill-conceived experiment gone terribly wrong. On the morning of April 26, 1986, those in charge of the site decided to see what would happen if some of the systems failed, so they deliberately shut down part of the reactor. Unfortunately, when certain systems slowed down, others suddenly sped up. This might not have been a problem if the plant had been carefully and properly built, but Chernobyl was built quickly to substandard specifications. In addition, widespread theft of materials had resulted in even poorer construction. Workers who needed cement for their own purposes often substituted sand as filler, resulting in foundations and walls that crumbled under pressure.

Within seconds of the shutdown, two earthquake-like shocks rolled through the building. Radioactive water started pouring through parts of the building, while others caught on fire. Only a handful of people were immediately killed or seriously injured, but firemen and other workers poured into the area to do what they could to contain the situation. Few wore any protective clothing, and thus many of them were exposed to lethal levels of radiation and died over the next few months. Altogether the amount of radiation leaked was three hundred times that of the atomic bomb dropped on Hiroshima, but because it happened over a longer period of time, the immediate death and injury rate was deceptively small at first, and as yet cannot be fully assessed.

The Soviet government initially ignored then later tried to cover up the accident. May 1 was the biggest Soviet holiday, and people spent all day outside while invisible radiation pummeled them. According to historian Anna Reid in *Borderland*, while informed Soviet officials secretly got their families as far away as possible on sudden, unscheduled vacations, unaware "families went shopping and walked their dogs; fishermen lugged their tackle off to the Prypyat River; couples sunbathed around the power station's cooling ponds. Football matches went ahead, as did sixteen outdoor weddings. Off-duty station workers who rang up the town hall asking for instructions were told that the fire was none of their business."

By the time President Gorbachev went public, and for the first time in history admitted that an error had occurred in the Soviet Union, the period of highest radiation had passed in the region. Much of the soil, however, is still too contaminated to allow for crops or human habitation. For a hungry country, though, even today the choice is sometimes between starving or eating crops grown illegally in the region, food that looks fine but in fact can kill.

immediately at Chernobyl, but the long-term effects on nearby residents are still revealing themselves in the form of cancers, human and livestock deformities, and radioactive crops. Even though the Soviet government eventually had to admit the extent of the disaster, death certificates in Ukraine were not legally allowed even to suggest radiation poisoning as a cause.

As with the deliberate starvation that occurred under Stalin, the Soviet government's handling of Chernobyl seemed a clear indication that the leadership of the Soviet Union did not have Ukrainians' best interests at heart. As a result, they were no longer willing to put up with repressive leaders like Shcherbytsky. Most Ukrainians wanted to go further than ridding themselves of Shcherbytsky and favored getting out of the Soviet Union altogether, but they were still divided as to whether Ukraine should remain Communist and whether it should maintain ties with Russia. Independence, it seemed, would have to remain far in the future while such issues were resolved.

The father of the first firefighter who entered Chernobyl after the accident grieves at his son's grave in Moscow's Mitinskoye cemetery.

INDEPENDENCE

Those who believed that Ukraine had time to think through its future before becoming independent were proven wrong within a few years of Chernobyl. Gorbachev's credibility had taken a beating when he tried to cover up and then downplay the nuclear accident, and he quickly stepped up his policies of glasnost and perestroika in order to show the world that he was serious about reform. He found, however, that when Soviet citizens were free to speak, they did not speak kindly about communism, the Soviet Union, or him.

In 1988, the Ukrainian Catholic Church, celebrating one thousand years of Christianity in Ukraine, held parades and other celebrations, sending the message that they would stay underground no longer. Following their lead, a new nationalist organization called Rukh was

Ninety percent of Ukrainians voted for independence in 1991, successfully severing all political ties with the Soviet Union.

founded. Rukh's membership included many of the leaders imprisoned by Shcherbytsky; they took positions calling for freedom of worship, support for basic human rights, an end to communism, the use of Ukrainian as the official language, and complete independence. Largely the result of the efforts of Rukh, Shcherbytsky was forced from office in 1989. In the 1990 elections that followed, other than in heavily Russian eastern Ukraine and Crimea, Rukh proved very popular, and ended up in control of the city councils of Lvov and Kiev.

Over the next few months, more and more people began to desert the sinking ship of the Soviet Union. Even the most Russified Ukrainians had to recognize that Ukraine might be better off alone. Likewise, even the most loyal Communist Party members came out in favor of independence, fearing that if they were perceived as supporting the government of the Soviet Union, Ukrainians might use their newfound power at the ballot box to vote communism out altogether. In July 1990, as a compromise between those favoring immediate independence and those reluctant to do so, the Ukrainian parliament cast a vote to remain within a reformed Soviet Union, but as a self-governing republic. This proved a short-lived compromise that satisfied no one.

Then in August 1991 in Moscow, hard-line Communists attempted to unseat Gorbachev. Though unsuccessful, the weakness at the core of Soviet leadership was now clear, and many Soviet republics immediately moved for independence. Following their example, Ukraine moved to sever its political ties with the Soviet Union altogether. The Communist Party was disbanded, and late in 1991 a national referendum was held to ratify a declaration of independence already passed by the Rada. Approximately 90 percent of all Ukrainians, regardless of political or ethnic ties, voted yes. Leonid Kravchuk, a former chairman of the Communist Party but a respected leader nonetheless, was elected Ukraine's first president.

The nation of Ukraine had finally been born. Many would argue that, despite being centuries in the making, it was still a premature birth. Now it remained to be seen if it could breathe on its own.

4

STAYING ALIVE: DAILY LIFE IN UKRAINE

When the Soviet Union collapsed, an entire way of life went with it. Though it had been difficult, it was at least familiar. For some, particularly the elderly and the poor, the past seems considerably rosier than it actually was; for others, particularly the young, the future seems brighter than it probably is. However, for most, the present is barely tolerable.

In the excitement of declaring Ukrainian independence, it seemed for a while as if the past might somehow be swept away, and a future without hunger and fear, a future where individual effort could bring great rewards, might take its place. The first decade of independence brought new problems, though, creating chaos along with opportunity and eroding the already minimal standard of living for many. Life for Ukrainians, regardless of location or ethnic background, is still very hard and more uncertain than in the past. Most Ukrainians are apprehensive about the future at the same time that they are glad to be rid of the oppression of the Soviet era.

THE COMMUNIST LEGACY

To understand how life has changed, it is essential to understand how it was. Communism is based on the idea that people should put the best interests of their communities ahead of their own personal well-being and desires. In practice, what this meant in the Soviet Union was that people were not allowed to own property or work for profit. The government owned everything, from factories to farms, from apartment buildings to grocery stores. People had an assigned workplace and usually assigned housing as well. They worked for the equivalent of pennies an hour, but had few expenses because housing and food were provided almost completely free of charge. A loaf of bread might cost the equivalent of a penny or two, and housing required only a token payment of somewhere around the equivalent of $3 a month. Unemployment was almost nonexistent, except for the disabled, mothers of young children, and the elderly, all of whom were taken care of through pensions. Workers knew that regardless of their level of performance they would never be fired because the government would have to shoulder the burden of finding them another job. Medical care and education were free; even at the university level, those who could gain admission attended at no charge and good students received a stipend covering some of the cost of housing and food.

The goal of communism is to provide adequately for everyone. This, at least in theory, eliminates both wealth and poverty, but it also removes the kinds of choices about one's life that people in the West, including the United States, take for granted. As a result of several generations of a Communist society, today's Ukrainians are not used to meeting their own needs and do not know how to survive by their own efforts. They do not fully understand what seems to outsiders to be a simple concept of earning a living wage and paying one's expenses from it. They are not used to the idea of paying

Because the Communist state provided jobs for all, few Ukrainians today know how to look for a job.

taxes. Many had never in their lives had to look for a job. Those who found employment with profit-oriented companies are discovering for the first time that they can be fired for poor work. People whose goal is to get rich find they can do so by cheating, bribery, and crime more easily than by any honest means. All of these changes have created enormous disruptions in daily life.

HOUSING

Urban Ukrainians generally live in apartments rather than detached houses. Many of these apartments were hastily constructed during the Khrushchev era in the late 1950s and early '60s, and thus are known across the former Soviet Union as "Khrushchevkas." Others are older buildings remodeled into the kinds of apartments the Communist leaders preferred as a means of keeping control of the population. Called communal apartments, generally they consisted of a number of small rooms, each housing a family in only a few hundred square feet of space, and kitchen and bathroom facilities shared by all the families in the apartment. Though the number of families in an apartment varied, there were often more than a dozen.

Destroying privacy was one of the goals of these buildings. Some designs required going through one family's space to get to another's. One could not protest such arrangements because the desire for privacy was equated with having something to hide. Communal kitchens were the norm not just because they were cheaper than constructing a private kitchen for each apartment but because they created a situation where neighbors might overhear conversations and, it was hoped, report disloyal statements or questionable activities to the authorities.

When the Soviet Union fell, people thought they could move out of such dismal living quarters, but this was not easy to do because other options were not available. Many people still live in communal apartments, although now they must pay much more in rent. Others, either families with cash or speculators trying to make a profit in the new Ukraine, have been able to buy all or part of a communal apartment building and convert it into private dwellings complete with their own bathrooms and kitchens. Still others live in buildings existing before the era of communal apartments, which already had

INSIDE A UKRAINIAN HOME

Meredith Dalton, author of *Culture Shock: Ukraine* and a former resident of the country, describes her experiences in a typical Ukrainian home.

One thing I've always enjoyed about Ukraine is that you won't find many homes, or even some parts of homes, that you might call unlivable. Homes that I've visited are eminently livable, lived-in, comfortable, and often a bit disorderly. Furnishings vary; the luckier homes may have a piano, and bookshelves are generally prominent and well stocked. I've encountered several homes with a wall-sized photograph resembling the backdrop of a late-night talk show that never changes regardless of the season. Rugs hanging on walls are both decorative and serve as insulation. I especially love that the furniture and space have multiple purposes: the living room or den becomes a bedroom, thanks to all those amazing chairs—to say nothing of the couches—that convert into beds; the writing table is also the dining table, and so on.

A particularly important room is the kitchen, which now for more Ukrainians is a private one.

In the Ukrainian kitchen, guests are treated like family—or at the very least as intimate friends. This point should not be taken lightly; in a culture accustomed to communal living, privacy and trust are at a premium. In the Soviet era, one learned to be very selective in choosing friends; only with your most trusted friends could you sit in the kitchen and speak a little more openly if you dared.

Dalton claims that Ukrainian homes reflect the inhabitants' overall perspective on the world.

Ukrainian homes reflect the personalities of their owners, which is to say they are unpretentious, practical and adaptive. [Ukrainians] are generally unapologetic that their floors are less well scrubbed than Westerners might be accustomed to; Americans would at least try to give excuses.

private kitchens and bathrooms. During the Communist era, people were crammed into these apartments based on a formula of square footage required per person. Many families avoided sharing space with strangers by inviting other family members to join them in their apartment. They are particularly fortunate today because they managed to hang on to what is now considered favorable living space.

Regardless of the kind of place in which one lives, even if it has been remodeled the likelihood is that the building is in poor repair due to its shoddy original construction, which makes roofs leak and floors sag. Poor maintenance makes plumbing back up, and hall corridors remain in darkness for months. In addition, because of the increased cost and limited availability of housing, many people still try to cram into living quarters meant to accommodate only a few people. Newlyweds often find no place to live and end up, sometimes for years, moving back in with parents and living in a corner of a room, with only a curtain or bookcase providing a measure of privacy. Divorced couples often discover they must continue to live in the same apartment because there is no other affordable or available choice. Although governmental constraints on privacy have been removed, practically speaking most people have as little privacy as ever.

The typical home in Ukraine is primitive by Western standards.

In the countryside, the situation is different. Though communal villages were built in some areas, collectivization did not always mean that people were removed from their ancestral villages. Rural families tended to live as before, in private, separate homes. These homes are generally still very rustic, typically having an outhouse in the backyard. Inside, there may be only a fire or small stove for cooking. Though land was acknowledged to belong to a family, it was not legally owned as that term is understood in the United States. Such ownership is now possible for the first time, but it brings with it risks and obligations that Ukrainians are not used to, such as losing the land to someone else by being unable to pay a debt, and being personally responsible for the cost of maintaining property.

Although individual families may have added what were once considered luxuries, such as a refrigerator, indoor plumbing, and a television, life in rural Ukraine is still fairly primitive by Western standards. Many rural Ukrainians feel that it is harder to survive now without the kind of governmental support to which they had been accustomed.

FOOD

Frugality is nothing new to Ukrainians. Hearty stews and soups, such as the famous beet soup known as *Borscht*, are common as either main dishes or first courses. Bread and other flour or grain-based foods such as dumplings and yeast pancakes called *blini* are also mainstays. Another traditional snack is *salo*, raw pork fat marinated in garlic. Sometimes called "Ukrainian chocolate," it is spread on bread and consumed as the traditional accompaniment to shots of vodka. The source of *salo* is the abundant supply of pigs, which, along with other livestock, are raised on many Ukrainian farms. Because Ukraine is near the Black Sea and has numerous rivers and lakes for fishing, the Ukrainian diet contains more protein than elsewhere in the former Soviet Union, but meat and fish are still too expensive (even when available) to be consumed every day.

To ensure that *salo* (and the accompanying vodka), bread, and other food is available, many rural farmers have gone back to their pre-Soviet ways, which means farming individually but being part of a community where mutual assistance is the norm. People have traditionally helped with neighbors' harvests if necessary, and shared their bounty with others in need. Relationships have always been considered essential to survival, and mutual help is a major factor in relationships. In rural villages, barter is more important than money; a person may trade eggs for butter or jam or for a nonfood item such as cloth or hardware. In this way, goods are distributed as needed, and people gain the satisfaction of knowing they have been able to help each other out.

Bartering is also a common way of getting what one needs in the cities as well. For instance, if someone receives a package of coffee as a gift or finds a bargain somewhere, he or she may go to the local open market and simply stand on the sidewalk trying to sell or trade all or part of it. The open market, or *rynok*, is an essential part of city life. It is not only the most reliable source of reasonably priced vegetables and other foods but also the best place to find bargains on items such as linens, clothing, books, electronic equipment, and bootleg recordings of popular music.

Some of the foods available in the *rynok* were grown on small farms called dachas. In the Soviet era, people living in a city were entitled to claim a small plot of land in the nearby countryside, on which they could plant a garden. Little communities of small houses surrounded by tidy rows of vegetables, chicken coops, and flower gardens quickly sprang up. Many families move to their dachas for the summer once school is over. After they have harvested their crops, they close up the dacha for the winter. A dacha is not what Westerners would think of as a summer home. It is not a luxury, and in fact the work to be done can be grueling. Often the products of the dacha are what keep the family alive through the long winter in the city.

Ukrainians also love to gather socially, throughout the year, especially in the winter when nights are long and there is less work to do. In both the cities and the villages, visitors are often astonished at the amount of food that seems to materialize from nowhere for a special occasion. Ukrainian hostesses usually have a hidden stash of canned or otherwise preserved food such as fruits, pickles, or meats, which they pull out for special occasions. Even when people get together casually, food will figure centrally, and some effort will be made to honor the occasion with a special treat. Particularly characteristic of Ukrainian cuisine are bite-size snacks

called *zakusky*. *Zakusky* may be nothing more than brown bread chunks with sausage or cheese, pickles, or salted herring, but can include caviar, smoked salmon, or other expensive treats.

According to writer Meredith Dalton, "most *zakusky* are salty, fatty, and spicy—considered an ideal accompaniment to alcohol,"[25] which to many Ukrainians is the true main course. Vodka is consumed in huge quantities in Ukraine, especially by men, who will rarely leave a quart-sized bottle unemptied and consider only three men sufficient for the task of emptying it. Alcoholism is a major health problem in Ukraine, as elsewhere in the former Communist nations. It has reduced the life expectancy for men to below sixty, as a result of diseases and accidental death, especially in car accidents and drownings. It is nearly impossible to avoid drinking vodka in Ukraine, almost always to the point of total drunkenness, because meals or other get-togethers with friends require numerous toasts, each of which requires a shot of vodka. Women are usually permitted to nurse a shot over several toasts, but both women and men are expected to toss

A Kiev marketplace draws residents who barter for or buy food, clothing, books, and other items.

down the first one. Alcoholism is not understood as a disease or a condition requiring abstinence, and refusal to participate in toasts is considered a major social error.

HEALTH CARE

Indulgence in alcohol to the point of bodily harm is only one of the health issues confronting Ukraine today. Other major health problems include common infectious diseases. Many Ukrainians are not routinely immunized, and this causes much avoidable illness; more often, they fall seriously ill from diseases that are treatable with antibiotics. For example, a person with food poisoning or complications such as pneumonia from the flu or a cold may die before adequate medical care can be found.

Finding good care is a big problem. Doctors are so poorly paid that they often demand bribes, and hospitals are so stretched for operating funds that they may expect immediate payment of the entire bill. Supplies are inadequate, and it is nearly impossible to maintain the level of cleanliness required for surgery or inpatient care. Diseases such as AIDS often go

Poorly paid doctors, inadequate supplies, and lack of funding hamper efforts to provide high-quality health care.

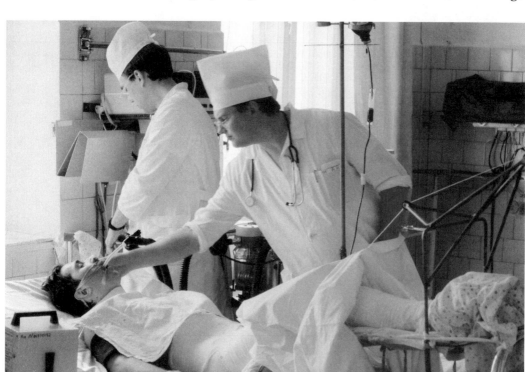

HORROR IN THE HOSPITAL

Ania Savage, an American journalist born in Ukraine, returned on several occasions in the 1990s to live for extended periods of time. On one of her visits she made friends with an American couple living in Kiev with their daughter Amber. One day Amber fell ill, and her subsequent brush with death, recounted in Savage's book *Return to Ukraine*, illustrates the problems with Ukrainian medical care.

Amber falls ill on a Thursday, and on Friday a doctor is summoned. He says she had probably eaten spoiled food and offers chamomile tea as a remedy. By Sunday evening Amber is very ill with vomiting and diarrhea, and a man living in their building offers to lay his hands on her to cure her. By the following Tuesday another doctor agrees to come to the house to see her. He too prescribes chamomile tea, and some tablets he does not identify. Savage recounts that "Amber is a very sick child. She is hardly moving, uninterested in her surroundings. She does not eat or drink. She is losing weight so rapidly that we can see her bones sticking out more and more as the day progresses." Another doctor is summoned, whose solution is to give Amber a tranquilizer to make her relax and stop crying.

Finally Amber is taken by ambulance to a hospital, reputedly the best in Kiev, where she is escorted through a garbage-strewn entry and put on a cot with a dirty sheet. According to Savage, her room "is a small, dirty hovel. Loose paint flakes in sheets from the ceiling." The bathroom has a toilet without a seat and a garden hose for taking a shower. Cockroaches scurry away when the lights are turned on. Frieda, Amber's mother, is periodically brought tea, but no fluids are given to Amber. Children can be heard crying in the other rooms, and when Frieda investigates she sees an unsupervised child hitting a smaller patient, and "a child sitting on the floor opening vials from an unlocked cupboard and drinking the contents."

"By dawn, Frieda knows what she must do: get Amber out of the hospital." She hurriedly dresses Amber and slips out into the alley behind the hospital to take her home on the trolley. Other American friends give Frieda antibiotics and drugs from their private stashes, and eventually Amber responds. A full month later, a health inspector visits their home to tell them the lab tests had finally been processed and Amber had salmonella poisoning. The family left Kiev soon after.

undiagnosed until they are past helping and others have been infected. Support services such as those provided by nurses, dietitians, and orderlies are not adequate. In many cases there are not enough staff members for the number of patients, and when the staff is available they are often poorly trained and even more poorly paid. The subsequent indifference to the patient's outcome kills many Ukrainians each year.

This lack of confidence in doctors, nurses, hospitals, and clinics is nothing new. Although medical care was free in the Soviet era, and in fact was one of the most loudly proclaimed success stories of communism, the truth was that it was woefully inadequate. The same problems of morale, training, pay, facilities, supplies, and other shortcomings that exist today were the norm then as well. As a result, Ukrainians, generally superstitious as a rule, have continued to seek medical help outside the hospitals and clinics. Herbal remedies and healers are popular, and in many cases may be equally or more effective than the substandard and often dangerous care received in hospitals.

EDUCATION

Schooling has also suffered in the years since the fall of communism. Although Ukraine is a well-educated country overall, with a nearly 100 percent literacy rate, the quality of education has declined as a result of the lack of funding for schools. As with nearly everything else in Ukraine, maintenance of schools was inadequate for decades, and school buildings tend to be dreary, uncomfortable places. This affects the morale of teachers and students alike, who spend days in poorly ventilated rooms with peeling paint and leaking ceilings, often using a few outdated textbooks for a whole class.

The problems with Ukrainian education run deeper than dry rot in the walls and water stains on the ceilings. Ukraine's long history of second-class status in relation to Russia resulted in a school curriculum that nearly completely ignored Ukraine and Ukrainians. The emphasis was on making good Soviet citizens of Ukrainians. Most Ukrainians are more comfortable with the Russian language than the Ukrainian one at this point, and many, especially in the east and Crimea, are ethnic Russian. Thus, even questions such as whether students should be taught in Ukrainian have become hot political issues. Those favoring school instruction in Ukrainian have prevailed, and today Russian is treated as a foreign language, along with English and several others. Similar heated arguments about the extent to which classes in Ukrainian history should include Russian history have not been resolved, and the slant in these classes varies from region to region and even teacher to teacher.

Children are generally unaware of the controversies swirling around them, and simply go to school and learn what they are taught without questioning its appropriateness. They begin school at age six and attend primary school for four years. After primary school they attend secondary school for at least five more years. Once they finish ninth grade, they receive a diploma. At that point they may leave school or continue for two more years of secondary education. Usually students leave after ninth grade unless they are preparing to enter a university or one of the many technical colleges that require extra secondary coursework. Some students leaving after ninth grade immediately look for employment, but others go to trade schools to get skills in such things as cooking or printing.

Today there are approximately fifteen universities in Ukraine, although some are new and not yet accredited. Competition for acceptance to the major universities is stiff, but poor faculty pay and deteriorating conditions have made them no longer the internationally respected institutions they once were. One exception to this decline is in computer technology. Ukraine has kept pace with the electronic age, and computer literacy, among the well educated at least, is high. Even though chaos in today's Ukraine, coupled with the difficulties of finding highly paid professional work, has made many young people question whether pursuing higher education is worthwhile, universities are well attended in some fields, including business and computer science.

WORK

The confusion and uncertainty of life in today's Ukraine is reflected in the workplace as well. Today, salaries for most Ukrainians are generally well under what is necessary for survival, and even these salaries are irregularly paid. As a result, in Ukraine the shadow economy is what keeps food on many tables. *Shadow economy* is the term used for business activities that take place outside the control of the government. Some are illegal because they are criminal, such as theft or

Many Ukrainians supplement their meager incomes by regularly pilfering company supplies for resale.

drug trade. Others are illegal because they are done without paying taxes, such as selling goods on the black market.

Though Ukrainians generally look for official paying jobs with the government or in privately owned businesses, many see these official jobs as safety nets and put most of their energy into other ways of making money. One popular way of supplementing income is to travel in search of bargains, which can be taken somewhere else and sold for a profit. In some cases this might consist of moving a surplus from one part of the city to another where the same goods are in short supply, or going into the countryside to buy extra produce to sell in the local market. In other cases, people travel across the border to Poland or another neighboring country, spend several days collecting goods, then smuggle their purchases back across the border to sell in Ukraine.

Those with official jobs often see their employment not as an end in itself but as a means by which they can supplement their income in other ways. Pilfering of supplies is rampant regardless of whether one works in a construction yard or a government office. Bricks, nails, paper, pens, and whatever else is stealable ends up in the shadow economy as something to either barter or sell. Salable goods, however, are not the only thing of value in today's Ukraine. Another reason to have a regular job is to have what is known in Russian as *blat*. *Blat*, which roughly translates as clout, or pull, is the influence an insider possesses. Those who work in an office, for example, may be able to help find a job for a neighbor. They may find a way to put a friend or relative's application for a governmental permit (which are usually required at each step of even the simplest processes) on the top of the pile, saving months or years of waiting. This creates an obligation that will be repaid in the future in some fashion. For many Ukrainians, *blat* may be their most precious asset. These networks of obligation, rather than laws or government-imposed structure, are seen by many sociologists as the hidden threads that hold together today's Ukraine.

Ukrainians work much harder outside their official jobs than they do during working hours. This in part is a result of the Soviet era when, to maintain full employment, the government often had far more workers than it actually needed in factories and offices. Since there was not enough work to do, the workers expected their day to include long breaks and a very slow work pace. Thus, in present-day Ukraine, most don't feel obligated to help their employers do well and continue to go through their work days with often deliberate inefficiency, partly as a way of getting back for inadequate and irregular wages and partly because that is simply the way it has always been. Clearly, such a way of life, both in formal employment and in the shadow economy, wastes enormous amounts of time and energy.

REST AND RELAXATION

The average Ukrainian adult lives in a state of perpetual exhaustion. It requires constant hustling to keep a family clothed and fed. In addition, one must maintain networks of favors by putting energy into helping others. Survival is a seven-day-a-week job. As the government and other large employers become less and less able to pay their staffs, the number of holidays has increased as compensation, but this situation has only served to underscore how small a part formal jobs really have in the lives of Ukrainians.

Holidays often mean little more than shadow economy business as usual. In part this is because Ukrainian holidays evoke mixed feelings among the population. In the post–Soviet era, many important holidays, such as Soviet Army Day, are no longer celebrated at all, but attempts to create new holidays have not been very successful, largely because Ukrainians do not always agree about what should be celebrated. A few new holidays, such as a day of National Mourning in September honoring everyone who died in the political upheavals and wars of the twentieth century, are growing in importance. Most days off are treated as chances to stay home and rest, or to go out and make a little more money.

Still, life is not all dreariness and work. Family events such as weddings are times for tables to overflow with all the best *zakusky* and other delicious fare. Traditional music is played, and vodka toasts follow so close to each other that everyone staggers home. Such events are held both in rural villages and in the cities, but the cities have additional outlets for recreation. Most notable among these is the annual music festival Chervona Ruta, named after the title of a popular modern Ukrainian love song. The first Chervona Ruta festival was held in 1989, before independence, in the western region of Chernivtsi.

Designed to promote the idea of an independent Ukraine by focusing on patriotic and traditional music, the Chervona Ruta festival has continued since independence, funded in

A mother and her children celebrate the Russian Orthodox Christmas at a carnival in Kiev.

large part by the government, which sees its value in creating a Ukrainian identity. Chervona Ruta pulls together all aspects of Ukrainian culture, opening usually with blessing rituals by priests of the various Ukrainian churches. All music must be in Ukrainian, and Ukrainian themes must be part of each group's performance. The festival ranges from traditional to punk and heavy metal groups, including a group known as the Snake Brothers, whose song "We're the Boys from Banderstadt" ("We go to church/We respect our parents/No one can party like us/Till the bugles don't play/Till the drum doesn't beat"[26]) brought down the house in the first festival after independence. Festivals like Chervona serve as a symbol for the new Ukraine. New, exciting, and focused on change but strongly reflective of tradition, these festivals are expressions of the energy and determination of Ukrainians—qualities they will continue to need in the years to come as they struggle to improve their daily lives.

5

"UKRAINE IS NOT YET DEAD": CONTEMPORARY CHALLENGES

The title of Ukraine's national anthem, "Ukraine Is Not Yet Dead," is a far cry from typical anthem themes of victory in battle and the eternal greatness of one's country. When Ukrainians utter the words "Luck will still smile on us brother-Ukrainians," they are singing about their hopes for a happier, freer, and more bountiful future. When they sing "we'll prove that we brothers are of Cossack kin,"[27] they are giving voice to their pride in those few chapters in their past where they seemed to be in charge of their own destiny.

Hope and a fragile sense of national history are two of the things Ukrainians are able to cling to, and though the anthem's modesty and somewhat negative undertones may cause some amusement for foreign listeners, it is an accurate reflection of many Ukrainians' feelings about their country. For today's Ukrainians, survival is accomplishment enough, and an anthem that implied otherwise would sound hollow. But the nation must find a way to do more than stagger from one day to the next. If Ukraine is to stabilize and progress, it will take more than luck and a vague sense of common Cossack brotherhood to make this happen.

THE TANGLED WEB OF MONEY

In today's Ukraine it is difficult to determine how to go about addressing any individual problem because each problem seems to be interwoven with every other problem imaginable. For example, most of the problems of today's Ukraine can be traced back in one way or another to money. To understand how a lack of familiarity with money affects Ukrainians' daily lives, it is important to think for a minute how much Americans take for granted about getting, having, and spending money. In the United States people can generally rely on their paychecks being ready on payday, and the amount can be predicted from the number of hours worked or from one's regular salary. People also have a reasonably good idea about the buying power of their paychecks: how much food, clothing, rent, transportation, and other things are going to cost. It would not occur to most Americans to offer a bribe to someone at the supermarket to do them a favor like hiding, stealing, or undercharging for an item. These common understandings—that paychecks will be on time, that prices will not double overnight, that bribes are not required to get

"UKRAINE IS NOT DEAD YET"

The Ukrainian national anthem, quoted by Meredith Dalton in *Culture Shock: Ukraine,* reflects not only Ukrainians' pride in their country but also an acknowledgment of the difficulties of Ukraine's past—and the uncertainty of its future.

Ukraine is not yet dead, nor its glory and freedom,

Luck will still smile on us brother-Ukrainians.

Our enemies will die, as the dew does in the sunshine,

And we, too, brothers, we'll live happily in our land.

We'll not spare either our souls or bodies to get freedom

And we'll prove that we brothers are of Cossack kin.

We'll rise up brothers, all of us, from the Sain to the Don,

We won't let anyone govern in our motherland.

The Black Sea will smile yet, Grandfather Dnipro will rejoice,

Yet in our Ukraine luck will be high.

Our persistence, our sincere toil will prove its rightness,

Still our freedom's loud song will spread throughout Ukraine.

It will reflect upon the Carpathians, will sound through the steppes,

And Ukraine's glory will arise among the people.

what one wants—make daily life go fairly smoothly. Likewise, most Americans feel their money is safe in the bank, and though they may not want to pay taxes, most see it as inevitable. These things are new to Ukrainians, most of whom have never written a check or paid money to the government in the form of taxes. They don't know what the rules for anything are because there are no clear rules. They don't know what their rights are because no consistent set of rights exists. Even the simple concept of working for a paycheck and then living on however little or much one makes is new to Ukrainians.

After the fall of communism, people suddenly had to have money, but the means to get it were not in place. There were no existing standards to determine how much people should make on the job and no laws to keep employers from underpaying or not paying at all or to keep employees from taking matters into their own hands. Even today, a decade later, the government often does not meet its payroll, leaving employees with nothing on payday. As a result, employees feel no

A bus factory worker is just one of many Ukrainians who cannot count on getting paid each payday.

qualms about such things as clocking in to one job and then leaving to work another job for most of the day or systematically stealing materials and supplies from their employers and then selling them or trading them on the black market. Getting, having, and spending money in Ukraine has become not just an economic issue but also a legal one, as the government finds itself unable to establish and enforce laws. Both petty and serious crime have skyrocketed, as people do whatever they feel they must to get money they need to survive.

The need for money has also filtered into other aspects of life in Ukraine. For example, the need to have jobs to pay for food and shelter for one's family has kept open industrial plants that pollute the environment and cause sickness in those who fight the hardest against closing them—the workers who depend on the income from the plants. Others continue to grow vegetables in soil known after Chernobyl to be radioactive, because they need the income from selling the vegetables. Thus, environmental issues also have become wrapped up with money.

Foreign trade and international relations in general are impacted by the monetary chaos in Ukraine, because without a stable economy, other countries lack the confidence to lend Ukraine badly needed money or to make big investments in its future by opening businesses there. It is clear that the government is not really running the country; rather, individual Ukrainians are simply doing whatever they must to live from day to day. Promises and glowing projections for the future made by the government don't mean very much.

The Economy

Getting control of the flow of money is an essential part of creating a stable, independent Ukrainian nation. This has been impossible so far because there is no clear agreement about what kind of economy Ukraine should have. The issue boils down to whether Ukraine should move as quickly as it can toward establishing a market economy or keep its economic system much as it was under the Soviet Union.

A market economy, such as that in the United States and Western Europe, is based on the idea that it is the individual business owner's responsibility to determine what people will want to spend money on, then figure out how to sell it to them at a profit. It is also based on the idea that business is

REPACKAGING CHERNOBYL

In the last few years of the Soviet Union, as a result of the policy of openness known as glasnost, textbooks in Soviet schools were openly critical of the government's handling of the 1986 nuclear accident at Chernobyl. According to anthropologist and political scientist Catherine Wanner in *Burden of Dreams: History and Identity in Post-Soviet Ukraine*, schoolchildren read of the "catastrophic ecological situation" that was "kept secret from the people." Some of the planners of the facility, site administrators, and government officials were identified by name and called criminals. One school text included this passage:

> The consequences of the Chernobyl accident, which will not be liquidated within the next few centuries, seem to be catastrophic for the whole planet, a tragedy for the whole world, affecting the fate of millions of people living on vast territories. Rivers, seas, oceans, and outdoor swimming pools of the planet already will never be the same as they were before Chernobyl.

Wanner points out that, less than a decade later, this passage about the need to bow to the authority of Moscow during the Soviet era contains the only reference to Chernobyl found in one new Ukrainian schoolbook: "One had to respond and support Moscow . . . even during the building of the Chernobyl Atomic Nuclear Station near Kiev, and even during indecision and even during cowardice as one of its reactors was built."

How could the event that most historians agree was the breaking point for the Soviet Union suddenly seem irrelevant to the country where it had occurred? The answer lies in the current economic situation: Ukraine simply cannot function without Chernobyl. Though the damaged reactor was shut down, the energy that lights up Kiev and the surrounding region still comes from the plant. Foreign aid, much of it from the United States, has enabled Ukraine to replace old facilities at Chernobyl with safer new ones, but going without nuclear energy is not an option for Ukraine. Now the government would like people to stop talking about the accident at Chernobyl. Apparently, the fears and indignation so important to turning Ukrainians against the Soviet government are not something the new government wants turned against itself.

risky, and those who are willing to take the risk of losing all the money they have invested in a restaurant, shop, or factory should be able to keep the profits if they make a success of it. Those who don't take the risk but remain in secure jobs working for other people give up the chance to become rich in exchange for a regular paycheck.

In a market economy, some are very rich and some are very poor, and most are in between. This is considered, rightly or wrongly, to be largely a matter of people's personal choices about their lives—how hard to work and how much risk to take—and thus their own concern, not society's. This is very different from the Communist system, in which everyone works for the good of the community and gets back for their labors what they need to survive. In the Communist era in Ukraine the emphasis was on getting by, existing at a barely adequate level. Today, however, for many Ukrainians getting by without having to work terribly hard is starting to seem like a luxury.

Many, particularly young adults and residents of western Ukraine, had stars in their eyes when the Communist Party fell from power. They were ambitious and energetic, willing to work hard to have the things money can buy. They favored as swift as possible a change to a market economy, and an

A woman compares prices in a Ukrainian market.

immediate severing of economic ties with Russia in favor of forging new links with Western Europe. As with so many other things, negative feelings about Russia motivated some to support whatever offered the clearest and most dramatic break with a country they despised. Others felt very differently, believing that the sudden fall of communism was a disaster and that steps should be taken to reinstitute it in an independent Ukraine. Some suggest that Ukraine should reunite with Russia in a new federation of equal partners. These views tend to be held by older Ukrainians, who are less able to deal with change and uncertainty after spending their lives under communism, and by those living in eastern Ukraine.

President Leonid Kravchuk imposed reforms designed to hasten separation from Russia.

CHAOS AT THE CORE

Such disagreements led to chaos for the government of independent Ukraine, aggravated by the fact that Ukraine was in no position to enter world markets. With independence, the

country's energy needs were no longer provided by the Soviet government at a fraction of their cost on the open market, and the machines and other products of Ukrainian factories were so out of date and shoddily made that no one would buy them. These realities had been hidden while the Soviet Union was intact because the machines were always taken off the factories' hands, and the oil and gas just kept arriving.

The first Ukrainian president, Leonid Kravchuk, reacted to this continued reliance on Russia by declaring that the transition to a market economy would need to be rapid so that a break with Russia could be made soon. The result was a spiraling inflation rate that reached 10,000 percent in 1993, as each business raised its prices to account for its higher costs and these costs were passed on to consumers. Just at the time when people were getting used to using money, no one had anywhere near enough of it to stay alive. Bartering, black market activities, and networks of family and friends were what got and continue to get the typical Ukrainian through life. Kravchuk tried to backpedal, but this only resulted in confusion. Halfhearted reforms seemed to make things worse than radical change or no change at all. Kravchuk was narrowly defeated in the 1994 elections by Leonid Kuchma, the current president of Ukraine.

Under Kuchma, inflation has been brought under control, largely as a result of slowing down the pace of reform and reaching agreements with Russia to keep some key costs such as gas and oil at artificially low levels. Ukraine agreed to let Russia keep its fleet in Black Sea harbors in exchange for forgiveness of its past-due payment on previously incurred debts for oil and gas, and for the continued receipt of these products at far below market value. Thus, the recent period of relative economic calm was not achieved by any real stability in the economy but by continuing to prop it up by hidden means.

Inflation is only one aspect of the economic picture in today's Ukraine. The government does not have the money it needs to function because it lacks the means to collect taxes. Even if a tax system were in place, it would not be able to collect much revenue because the black market and networks of family and friends function out of the sight and reach of the government. Because of its inadequate tax base, by 1997 the government owed $2.3 billion in back wages to its employees. Ukrainians who worked for the government had not been paid in months. People were not sure whether to direct their anger at the slow pace of reform or at the idea of reform in the first place. Those with the latter point of view began to support bringing back the Communist Party, and in the 1998 Rada parliamentary elections, the new Communist Party joined other parties with similar philosophies and together won one of every four votes cast in Ukraine. Today, the Communist and Communist-leaning members of the Rada have enough clout to stonewall legislation they do not like. The net result has been even greater ineffectiveness in government.

Government ineffectiveness has led to public unrest. In 1998, workers at a chemical plant near Lvov threatened to release poisonous waste into the Dniester River, and in 1999 workers at nuclear power plants threatened to cut off energy supplies to nearby cities. Both groups were protesting past-due wages. The presidential elections in 1999 saw a run-off between Kuchma and Petro Symonenko, whose Communist Party has made a strong comeback in Ukraine. In the end, Kuchma won a second term, with 60 percent of the vote, but it is apparent that the people of Ukraine are deeply divided about what kind of a future they want for their country.

CREATING A NATION OF LAWS

Economics is only one of the issues confronting today's Ukraine. It also must build a new legal system from scratch. Creating a nation of laws has several aspects. On the positive side, Ukraine has a constitution that is viewed as binding. The Rada is accepted as the legitimate legislative body, and Ukraine has managed to hold several presidential and parliamentary elections and abide by the results. Although the Rada may be ineffective, this is the result of disagreements among its members, not a lack of procedures for decision making. There is a sense that many in government are looking out for their own interests rather than the public's, but Ukraine does not seem to be on the verge of anarchy or revolution. People still look to the government to solve problems despite the fact that it has not been very effective.

Political scientist Paul D'Anieri, writing in *Politics and Society in Ukraine*, points out that, although "the crime rate is on the rise and corruption is rampant," signs of loss of faith

CORRUPTION AT THE TOP

Former prime minister of Ukraine Pavlo Lazarenko spent the year 2000 being held without bail in a California prison, awaiting trial for laundering $114 million in bribes received while in office. In 1998 in Ukraine, he was charged with stealing more than $2 million in state property and embezzling over $4 million from the state treasuries and laundering them through Swiss banks. He was arrested in December 1998 as he tried to enter Switzerland on a Panamanian passport, and in the summer of 2000, a Swiss court convicted him in absentia and seized $6.6 million from his bank accounts there.

Lazarenko's behavior is just the most recent in a series of scandals involving high officials. Anna Reid, writing in *Borderland*, says that "Corruption in high places is taken for granted. Eyebrows were scarcely raised when a former prime minister, Yuhym Zvyahilsky, fled to Israel in November 1994, accused of having pocketed tens of millions of dollars of public money via illegal oil exports." He came back three years later to serve as a deputy in the Rada, thanks to a self-serving vote by its members to make themselves immune from prosecution as long as they were actively serving in the parliament.

According to political scientist Paul D'Anieri in *Politics and Society in Ukraine*, the problem stems from "the general lack of a civic culture in Ukraine

[which] has produced a state where private concerns are routinely substituted for public welfare." The idea that government officials are public servants has clearly not yet taken hold in Ukraine. Top government officials, and their close friends, routinely take vacations and buy things such as cars and real estate that they could not possibly afford on their salaries, leaving many Ukrainians to believe that the government is in business for itself, not for them.

Former prime minister Pavlo Lazarenko is charged with stealing millions of dollars from Ukraine.

in the government's ability to run the country, such as riots, have not occurred and do not seem to be imminent. "Nonetheless, the government's policies *are* inconsistent and *do* lack coherence; they have been erratically formulated, poorly implemented, and selectively enforced."[28] Thus, while the president and the legislature struggle to find ways to assert their authority and begin necessary economic and other reforms, people continue to think that at least right now, life in Ukraine is a free-for-all.

This free-for-all has come about because it is not always clear who has the power to enforce existing laws. The distinct roles of the police, legislature, and courts have yet to be decided on. The laws in place are inadequate to deal with present-day reality, particularly in regard to property ownership and the operation of privately owned businesses. For example, laws regarding the sale of a home, a horse, or even a bushel of apples were not needed in the Soviet era because no one was allowed to own anything. Workplace regulations such as minimum wage and workplace safety laws were irrelevant because the government was in total control of everything and simply did what it saw fit. People might grumble, but there was no place to go to complain. For much of the Soviet era, a policy of "shoot first and ask questions later" took care of most lawbreakers, from petty thief on up. This fact, coupled with an unwritten understanding that officials of the Communist Party (and anyone else who could get away with it) were entitled to take advantage of their position by demanding bribes, has resulted in a culture where laws and official procedures are not taken seriously.

Today, the likelihood is that lawbreakers will not be punished. In fact it is often necessary to break existing laws to do business at all. If a person wants to get rich in today's Ukraine, he or she will almost certainly have to be some type of criminal to do it. An on-the-spot bribe of a customs official may get a carful of smuggled goods destined for the black market through a border checkpoint. A mugger can rest assured that if there is a police report it will probably remain indefinitely in the pile of papers on the desk of someone with little drive to address the injustice. An employer who underpays staff or a supplier whose produce is later discovered to be full of maggots is not likely to be held accountable because where to go and whom to talk to is unclear, because laws and punishments have not been established, or because red tape makes complaining time-consuming and ultimately pointless.

Violent crime in Ukraine is not as serious a threat to the stability of the nation as it is in Russia, but it is a growing problem. According to political scientist Ariel Cohen, "Ukraine is strategically located at the crossroads of the crime routes of Eurasia. Here smugglers of narcotics from the East meet car thieves from the West." The numerous armed conflicts in the region, including Bosnia and Kosovo, according to Cohen, have created a group of soldiers, merchants, and "outright bandits [who] made fortunes supplying weapons, ammunition, fuel, food, and other supplies."[29] In addition, lax security at nuclear plants has made theft of materials needed to make nuclear weapons a threat to the security of the world.

According to Paul D'Anieri, "Ordinary Ukrainians are able to sense the limits of state action"[30] and simply work around the state's ineffectiveness as they go about their daily lives. Daily life functions because people understand the importance of maintaining good relationships within their own networks, not because they are afraid of the reach of the law. If Ukraine is to progress toward an orderly society, though, it must develop a better legal system and the means of enforcing rules and regulations.

THE ENVIRONMENT

The major challenges affecting Ukraine's evolution—forming a national identity, developing a functioning economy, and creating a legal structure to govern the nation—touch upon almost every other aspect of life in today's Ukraine. From church to school to marketplace, the question of what kind of country they want to live in is always part of the picture for Ukrainians. Reconciling present-day reality with legacies of the past and hopes for the future is often very difficult, however, and this is nowhere better illustrated than in the environmental issues facing the nation.

As in many other Soviet bloc countries, industrialization in the twentieth century was accomplished with no concern for the effect on the environment. Countryside scarred by mining and smokestacks sending black plumes into the haze above cities were hailed as indications that the Soviet Union was catching up with the West, proof that communism was working. Polluted rivers were seen as a small price to pay for progress. Areas rich in natural resources, such as the Donbass in eastern Ukraine, became industrial centers, densely populated by workers needed in the new industries and mines.

When the Soviet Union fell, the sad economic realities of cities such as Donetsk and other industrial centers all over Ukraine became readily apparent. Production had been so inefficient that continued operation could only result in heavy monetary losses. The plants and mines could not be closed, however, because the resulting massive unemployment would threaten the stability of the country. In addition, no funds existed to retrofit or otherwise improve the plants to reduce their environmental pollution. Therefore, even though Ukrainians are now aware of how harmful pollution is to their health and to the future of their nation, there is little they can do about it. Factories continue to belch carcinogens and other poisons into rivers and the air. Maintenance of storage facilities for hazardous waste is so poor that more accidents of the sort at Chernobyl seem inevitable.

Still, such issues rank very far down on the list of worries of today's Ukrainians. Though many still attribute any health problems, crop failures, or other anomalies to fallout from Chernobyl, these occurrences are shrugged off as part of what must be endured, not something that should be addressed as a national priority. Likewise, other issues such as rampant discrimination against women in employment and the lack of adequate social services are rarely the focus of attention at all.

INTERNATIONAL RELATIONS

Ilya Prizel points out that "increasingly, countries around the world are coming to recognize Ukraine as an essential, integral part of Europe's security."[31] If the former Soviet bloc countries remain politically and economically unstable, Western Europe could find itself in a situation where a revitalized Russia is once again a threat. The solution, in the eyes of the United States and Western Europe, is to encourage Ukraine's view of itself as a European country, and to help Ukraine and other new post-Soviet nations become functioning democracies with healthy market economies.

Only in the past few years have Europe and the United States realized this. In the first years after independence, the United States focused almost exclusively on getting Ukraine to dismantle its nuclear weapons, not the issue of greatest

immediate Ukrainian concern. This resulted in an initially negative view of the United States as a potential ally, because it was perceived to have interests other than Ukraine's needs. When Ukraine did get rid of its nuclear arms in 1996, its relationship with the United States began to improve, however.

U.S. president Bill Clinton (left) and Ukraine president Leonid Kuchma (right) celebrate the signing of an agreement to close the Chernobyl nuclear facility.

In the last few years, beginning with separate visits by President Bill Clinton and Vice President Al Gore, the United States has begun to see the complexities and subtleties of Ukraine's problems, and economic and other forms of aid have been increased. According to political scientist Paula J. Dobriansky,

> While United States actions in the international arena make a difference, the success or failure of Ukraine's statehood will be largely determined by internal developments in Ukraine. In particular . . . the establishment of the rule of law [is] critical to Ukraine's independence. It is imperative for the United States to support strongly the development of democratic and free-market structures in Ukraine.[32]

Still, according to Paul A. Goble, "Ukraine's real resources in the West are in Europe,"[33] not the United States. Ukraine is no longer a borderland but a buffer zone between Russia and countries that have reason to fear Russia's centuries-old desire to expand its territory. Countries with particular reason to watch what happens in Ukraine are its immediate neighbors, such as Romania, Moldavia, Azerbaijan, and Georgia, which face similar challenges overhauling their societies after the fall of communism. Forming strong alliances with other countries trying to establish economic independence from Russia could result in greater stability for the whole region. For example, Ukraine is working with Georgia and Azerbaijan to create corridors for transporting oil that would avoid the use of the Caspian Sea, which Russia controls.

But Ukraine cannot simply ignore the fact of its proximity to Russia and its historical and economic ties to that country. For true stability in the region, it will need to find a way to stand shoulder to shoulder with Russia as equals. If Ukraine can join the West but still honor its links to Russia, it will truly become no longer a borderland but one of the most important nations in the modern world.

A THREEFOLD CHALLENGE

In the words of Ilya Prizel, "The emergence of Ukraine in 1991 as an independent state was as sudden as it was unexpected."[34] Its first challenge was the simple fact of independence, the realization that there was no longer the equivalent of a parent to look to for solutions to crises as well as for everyday needs. Immediate problems were too complex to be resolved quickly, and the ongoing confusion has made the country unable to become the post-Communist success story many had projected it would be.

The first challenge for Ukraine is to shift from a Communist to a market economy. The second is to change from a society where order was maintained by governmental intimidation to one of due process, where laws are clearly stated and evenly applied. The third is to develop a sense of identity, a belief that Ukraine is a legitimate separate country and that its people constitute one Ukrainian nation. These three things would be difficult enough to handle one at a time, but have so far proven impossible to handle at once. A smoothly functioning legislature and legal system would be able to proceed in an organized fashion to make economic reforms. A solid economy would create the kind of general social calm that would promote more thoughtful discussions and decision making among lawmakers about what laws were needed and how to enforce them. If these two elements were in place, it would be easier for Ukrainians to see themselves as one people working together, proud of their ability to build a nation. The better Ukraine functions in the future, the easier it will be for everyone to feel part of it.

In the words of Meredith Dalton, "Ukraine is not for the meek."[35] It takes a great deal of fortitude to go out every day to face a world that can seem to change overnight, where the problems are so burdensome and so complex they defy even the most sincere efforts to solve them. Although a review of Ukrainian history might lead to the conclusion that Ukrainians are easily overwhelmed by powerful forces, in fact the opposite is true. Ukrainians seem to be unbreakable, even in the face of calamities on the scale of Babi Yar, the Great Famine, and Chernobyl. Their perseverance in a situation that Paula J. Dobriansky calls "critical, but not hopeless"[36] is perhaps the most powerful resource they have today. As their anthem declares, someday "we too, brothers, we'll live happily in our land."[37]

Facts About Ukraine

Government

Government type: Republic

Capital: Kiev (2.6 million inhabitants)

Other major cities: Kharkov (1.6 million); Dnipropetrovsk (1.1 million); Donetsk (1.1 million); Odessa (1.1 million); Zaporizhzhya (890,000); Lvov (800,000)

Administrative divisions: Twenty-four regions called oblasts; one autonomous region (Crimea); two municipalities with blast status (Kiev, Sevastopol)

Independence: 1991, from Soviet Union; Independence Day celebrated August 24

Executive branch: President: Leonid Kuchma (since 1994); Prime minister: Valeriy Pustovoytenko (since 1997); Cabinet: appointed by president and approved by Supreme Council

Legislature: Supreme Council (Verkhovna Rada), a one-house unicameral) 450-seat legislature; half the seats allocated to parties reaching 4 percent threshold in elections, in proportions based on percentage of votes received; half the seats directly elected; members serve four-year terms

Next election: 2002

Judicial branch: Supreme Court; Constitutional Court

Geography

Location: Eastern Europe, bordering the Black Sea, between Poland and Russia

Area: 603,700 square km. (slightly smaller than Texas)

Bordering countries: Belarus, Hungary, Moldavia, Poland, Romania, Russia, Slovakia

Climate: Temperate continental; precipitation varies by region; winters vary from cool along the Black Sea to cold inland; summers vary from warm in most parts to hot in the south

Terrain: Fertile plains (steppes); mountains in the west and in Crimea; highest elevation, Hora Hoverla (2,061 meters)

Natural resources: Iron ore, coal, natural gas, oil, salt, sulfur, various metals, timber

Land use: Arable land: 58%; Pastures: 13%; Forest and woodland: 18%;

Other: 11%

Environmental issues: Lack of potable water; air and water pollution; deforestation; radiation contamination

PEOPLE (1999 FIGURES)

Population: 49 million

Population distribution: Urban: 68%; Rural: 32%

Age structure: 0–14: 18%; 15–64: 68%; 65+: 14% (more than twice as many women as men)

Population growth: –0.62%; Birth rate: 9.54 per 1000 population; Death rate: 16.38 per 1,000; Migration rate: .63 immigrants per 1,000

Infant mortality rate: 21.73 deaths per 1,000 live births

Life expectancy at birth: 65.91 years; males: 60.23 years; females: 71.87 years

Total fertility rate: 1.34 children born per woman

Ethnic groups: Ukrainian: 73%; Russian: 22%; Jewish: 1%; Other: 4%

Literacy (those over age 15 who can read and write): 98%

ECONOMY

Currency: Hryvnya (HRN); Value (mid-2000 figure): 5.4 HRN per U.S. dollar

Gross domestic product (GDP): $108.5 billion

GDP growth rate: –1.7%

GDP per capita: $2,200

GDP by sector: Agriculture: 14%; Industry: 30%; Services: 56%

Population below poverty line: 50%

Labor force: 22.8 million; Industry/construction: 32%; Agriculture/forestry: 24%; Health and education: 17%; Trade: 8%; Transportation and communication: 7%; other: 12%

Budget:Revenues: $18 billion; Expenditures: $21 billion

Industries: Coal, electric power, metals, machinery/vehicles, chemicals, sugar and other food processing

Industrial growth rate: –1.5%

Agricultural products: Grain, sugar beets, sunflower seeds, vegetables, beef, milk

Exports: $11.3 billion; Commodities: Metals, chemicals, machinery/vehicles, food products; Main partners: Russia, China, Turkey, Germany, Belarus

Imports: $13.1 billion; Commodities: Energy, machinery and parts, equipment, chemicals, plastics, rubber; Main partners: Russia, Germany, United States, Poland, Italy

NOTES

INTRODUCTION: THE BEWILDERED GIANT

1. Ania Savage, *Return to Ukraine.* College Station: Texas A&M University Press, 2000, p. 177.

2. Savage, *Return to Ukraine*, pp. 99–100.

CHAPTER 1: THE LAND AND PEOPLE OF UKRAINE

3. Ryan Ver Berkmoes et al., *Russia, Ukraine, and Belarus.* Melbourne, Australia: Lonely Planet, 2000, p. 875.

4. Ver Berkmoes et al., *Russia, Ukraine, and Belarus*, p. 842.

5. Ver Berkmoes et al., *Russia, Ukraine, and Belarus*, p. 807.

CHAPTER 2: FROM CONQUERORS TO CONQUERED

6. Meredith Dalton, *Culture Shock: Ukraine.* Portland, OR: Graphic Arts Center, 2000, p. 37.

7. Daniel C. Diller, *Russia and the Independent States.* Washington, DC: Congressional Quarterly, 1993, p. 290.

8. Quoted in Anna Reid, *Borderland: A Journey Through the History of Ukraine.* Boulder, CO: Westview Press, 1997, p. 10.

9. Quoted in Reid, *Borderland*, p. 12.

10. Ver Berkmoes et al., *Russia, Ukraine, and Belarus*, p. 718.

11. Reid, *Borderland*, p. 32.

12. Quoted in Reid, *Borderland*, p. 39.

13. Quoted in Reid, *Borderland*, p. 55.

14. Reid, *Borderland*, p. 97.

15. Quoted in Reid, *Borderland*, p. 100.

16. Quoted in Reid, *Borderland*, p. 100.

17. Reid, *Borderland*, p. 100.

CHAPTER 3: FROM SOVIET REPUBLIC TO INDEPENDENT NATION

18. Tim Smith et. al., *Ukraine's Forbidden History.* Stockport, England: Dewi Lewis, 1998, p. 9.

19. Quoted in Reid, *Borderland,* p. 106.

20. Ver Berkmoes et al., *Russia, Ukraine, and Belarus,* p. 720.

21. Quoted in Smith et al., *Ukraine's Forbidden History,* p. 11.

22. Ver Berkmoes et al., *Russia, Ukraine, and Belarus,* p. 721.

23. Smith et al., *Ukraine's Forbidden History,* p. 11.

24. Diller, *Russia and the Independent States,* p. 292.

CHAPTER 4: STAYING ALIVE: DAILY LIFE IN UKRAINE

25. Dalton, *Culture Shock: Ukraine,* p. 175.

26. Quoted in Catherine Wanner, *Burden of Dreams: History and Identity in Post-Soviet Ukraine.* University Park: Pennsylvania State University Press, 1998, p. 130.

CHAPTER 5: "UKRAINE IS NOT YET DEAD": CONTEMPORARY CHALLENGES

27. Quoted in Dalton, *Culture Shock:Ukraine,* p. 263.

28. Paul D'Anieri, Robert Kravchuk, and Taras Kuzio, *Politics and Society in Ukraine.* Boulder, CO: Westview Press, 1999, p. 140.

29. Quoted in Sharon L. Wolchik and Volodymyr Zviglyanich, ed. Lanham, MD: Rowman and Littlefield, *Ukraine: The Search for a National Identity,* pp. 292, 293.

30. D'Anieri, et al., *Politics and Society in Ukraine,* p. 140.

31. Quoted in Wolchik and Zviglyanich, *Ukraine,* p. 27.

32. Quoted in Wolchik and Zviglyanich, *Ukraine,* p. 129.

33. Quoted in Wolchik and Zviglyanich, *Ukraine,* p. 113.

34. Quoted in Wolchik and Zviglyanich, *Ukraine,* p. 13.

35. Dalton, *Culture Shock: Ukraine,* p. 263.

36. Quoted in Wolchik and Zviglyanich, *Ukraine,* p. 129.

37. Quoted in Dalton, *Culture Shock: Ukraine,* p. 263.

GLOSSARY

anti-Semite: Someone who dislikes Jews.

collective: A large holding, such as a farm, put together from many smaller holdings and operated under government supervision.

communism: A system of government in which private property is abolished and goods (and the means to produce them, such as land, industries, etc.) are owned by the state, which makes them available to all as needed.

Cyrillic: The alphabet used to write Russian and Ukrainian.

dacha: A summer cottage with a small plot of land used by city families to grow vegetables and other food for the winter.

deportation: The act of sending a person out of a country on the grounds that he or she is there illegally.

glasnost: "Openness" in Russian; the policy of honesty advocated by Mikhail Gorbachev in the last years of the Soviet Union.

gulag: A prison camp.

hetman: Cossack term for ruler.

kolkhoz: Russian word for collective farm.

kulak: A "wealthy peasant," one who had even slightly more than neighbors. "Dekulakization" was the term coined by Joseph Stalin when he began having kulaks killed as enemies of the state.

market capitalism/market economy: Terms used to describe an economic system based on supply and demand in which businesses are privately owned, not operated by the government.

nationalist: A person who advocates the creation of a nation or strengthening the sense of national unity of an existing one.

Orthodox: Referring to the practices of Christians in Eastern Europe and Central Asia, as distinct from Roman Catholics or Protestants.

perestroika: Russian for "restructuring;" the attempts made by Mikhail Gorbachev in the last years of the Soviet Union to allow privatization of business, open elections, and other reforms.

principality: A territory ruled by a prince.

Rada: Cossack term for council, now used as the name of the Ukrainian legislature.

Russification: The process by which Ukrainians were made to think of themselves as part of Russia.

rynok: Ukrainian word for market.

serfdom: A form of slavery in which people are seen as belonging to a particular piece of land, and hence owned by the landowner.

shadow economy: Buying and selling that takes place out of the control of the government; both black market activity and informal networks of barter and sale are part of the shadow economy.

Sovietification: The process by which Ukrainians were made to see themselves as Soviet citizens and see Ukraine as a Soviet republic.

steppe: Generally flat prairie land characterized by a lack of trees.

Ukrainianization: The process by which people are made to think of themselves as citizens of the nation of Ukraine.

zakusky: Snack.

CHRONOLOGY

Seventh Century B.C.
Greeks and Scythians establish colonies in Ukraine.

Sixth Century A.D.
Slavs settle in Ukraine.

Eighth Century
Khazars become the most powerful group in Ukraine.

Ninth Century
Varangians (Vikings) create trading posts along the Dnieper River.

CA. 900
Oleh the Wise brings the Ukrainian regions together into one kingdom.

988
Prince Volodymyr converts to Christianity and is baptized.

1037
Construction of Santa Sofia Cathedral is completed in Kiev.

1054
Yaroslav the Wise divides Kievan Rus among his sons, leading to its decline.

1240
Mongols, led by Batu, occupy Kiev.

Fifteenth Century
Cossacks establish first communities in southern and eastern Ukraine.

1553
The most important Cossack community, Zaporizky Sich, is founded.

1569
Union of Lublin unites Poland and Lithuania into one nation.

1648
Beginning of the Khmelnytsky Rebellion.

1654
Khmelnytsky forms an alliance with Russia.

1657–1686
Period of warfare called the "Ruin" by Ukrainians.

1667
Russian-Polish treaty gives land east of theDnieper River to Russia.

1773
First partition of Poland gives Galicia to Austria.

1795
Third partition of Poland cedes remaining portions of Polish Ukraine to Russia.

1876
Edict of Ems bans teaching and publishing in the Ukrainian language.

1917
Russian tsar Nicholas II abdicates; Bolshevik coup follows.

1918
Treaty of Brest-Litovsk.

1918–1921
Civil war for control of Ukraine.

1919
Treaty of Versailles gives control of western Ukraine to Poland.

1921
Treaty of Riga establishes the border between the Soviet Union and Poland with no input from Ukraine.

1927
Joseph Stalin becomes the leader of the Soviet Union.

1929
Collectivization and dekulakization begins.

1932–1933
Deliberate starvation campaign in Ukraine.

1937–1939
Second campaign of purges.

1939
Molotov-Ribbentrop Pact results in Soviet occupation of Galicia; the current western border of Ukraine is established.

1941
Germany invades Ukraine.

1942
Ukrainian Insurgent Army is established.

1943–1944
Soviet army reestablishes control in Ukraine.

1972
Volodymyr Shcherbytsky becomes the head of the Ukrainian communist party.

1985
Mikhail Gorbachev becomes the leader of the Soviet Union.

1986
World's worst nuclear accident occurs at Chernobyl.

1987
Political prisoners freed by Gorbachev return to Ukraine.

1989
Shcherbytsky is forced to resign; Rukh is founded.

1991
Attempted coup by hard-line Communists against Mikhail Gorbachev; Ukraine declares independence; Leonid Kravchuk is elected the first president.

1994
Leonid Kuchma is elected the second president of independent Ukraine.

SUGGESTIONS FOR FURTHER READING

BOOKS

John Channon, *The Penguin Historical Atlas of Russia.* London: Penguin Books, 1996. Although the book traces Russian history, its excellent maps and explanations include much useful information about Ukraine.

Joyce Moss and George Wilson, *Peoples of the World: Eastern Europe and the Post-Soviet Republics.* Detroit: Gale Research, 1993. Encyclopedia-like entries on a few older regional cultures such as the Cossacks, modern ethnic groups, and basic country information.

Tim Smith et al., *Ukraine's Forbidden History.* Stockport, England: Dewi Lewis, 1998. Excellent photo essay focusing on the suffering and repression of the Ukrainian people from the 1920s until the fall of the Soviet Empire.

WEBSITES

Brama-Gateway Ukraine (www.brama.com). Comprehensive site for news, travel and business information, and other resources. Most articles are in both Ukrainian and English.

Day (www.day.kiev.au). Although this Kiev-based site itself is in Ukrainian, a weekly news digest in English covers the economy, politics, culture, and other topics.

Ukraine (http://physics.mcgill.ca). This site from an expatriate Ukrainian calling himself simply Oleh maintains the best and most thorough collection of links to a wide range of websites.

Works Consulted

Books

Simon Broughton et al., *World Music: The Rough Guide.* London: Rough Guides, 1994. The definitive source of information on contemporary world music, including a section on Ukraine.

Meredith Dalton, *Culture Shock: Ukraine.* Portland, OR: Graphic Arts Center, 2000. From the *Culture Shock* series, this volume offers explanations of various aspects of the Ukrainian way of life.

Paul D'Anieri, Robert Kravchuk, and Taras Kuzio, *Politics and Society in Ukraine.* Boulder, CO: Westview Press, 1999. A series of scholarly essays on different aspects of life in today's Ukraine.

Karen Dawisha and Bruce Parrott, *Russia and the New States of Eurasia: The Politics of Upheaval.* Cambridge, England: University of Cambridge Press, 1994. Excellent and thorough book covering history, economics, and politics in countries of the former Soviet Union.

Daniel C. Diller, *Russia and the Independent States.* Washington, DC: Congressional Quarterly, 1993. A historical book with many good photographs and explanatory sidebars.

Anatol Lieven, *Ukraine and Russia: Fraternal Rivalry.* Washington, DC: U.S. Institute of Peace Press, 1999. Journalist Lieven explores the complex links between Russia and Ukraine.

Anna Reid, *Borderland: A Journey Through the History of Ukraine.* Boulder, CO: Westview Press, 1997. A well-written and unusual combination of history and contemporary analysis, focusing on a few cities and regions.

Ivan L. Rudnytsky, *Essays in Modern Ukrainian History.* Cambridge, MA: Harvard University Press, 1987. Although published before Ukraine's independence, this book contains a number of insightful and still valid analyses.

Ania Savage, *Return to Ukraine*. College Station: Texas A&M University Press, 2000. Acclaimed memoir of a journalist returning to Ukraine.

Theodore Shabad, *Geography of the USSR: A Regional Survey*. New York: Columbia University Press, 1951. An older book, this work contains descriptions of the land of today's Ukraine.

Stephen Velychenko, *Shaping Identity in Eastern Europe and Russia*. New York: St. Martin's Press, 1993. This scholarly work contains a great deal of information focusing on Ukraine during the Soviet era.

Ryan Ver Berkmoes et al., *Russia, Ukraine, and Belarus*. Melbourne, Australia: Lonely Planet, 2000. A guidebook designed for tourists and others interested in Ukraine, this work contains a substantial and informative section on Ukrainian history and sights.

Catherine Wanner, *Burden of Dreams: History and Identity in Post-Soviet Ukraine*. University Park: Pennsylvania State University Press, 1998. Excellent scholarly work on the Soviet legacy and recent developments in Ukraine's transition.

Sharon L. Wolchik and Volodymyr Zviglyanich, eds., *Ukraine: The Search for a National Identity*. Lanham, MD: Rowman and Littlefield, 2000. A series of scholarly essays about Ukraine's emerging identity and the challenges of nation building.

WEBSITES

Ukraine Today Weekly (www.ukrainet.Lvov.ua). Lvov-based news service with archives going back several years.

Willard Group, Ukraine Observer (www.ukraine-observer.com). Good on-line magazine focusing on topics of interest to businesspeople.

INDEX

PICTURE CREDITS

Cover photo: © Photri Inc.
© AFP/Corbis, 76, 91
© AP Photo/Efrem Lukatsky, 83, 87
© AP Photo/Eric Risberg, 56
© Archive Photos, 19, 45, 53
© Craig Aurness/Corbis, 25
© Fabienne Bouville/Impact Visuals, 69
© Corbis-Bettmann, 14
© Jay Dickman/Corbis, 74
© Dave G. Houser/Corbis, 21
© Hulton Getty/Archive Photos, 39, 41, 49, 52, 55
© Ed Kashi/Corbis, 8, 26
© Yevgeny Khadlei/Corbis, 46
© Caroline Penn/Corbis, 66
© Popperfoto/Archive Photos, 37
© Reuters/Eric Miller/Archive Photos, 84
© Reuters/Unknown/Archive Photos, 59
© Sean Sprague/Impact Visuals, 7
© Stock Montage, 29
© David Turnley/Corbis, 63, 70
© Peter Turnley/Corbis, 11, 60, 80
© Nik Wheeler/Corbis, 17, 23

ABOUT THE AUTHOR

Laurel Corona lives in Lake Arrowhead, California, and teaches English and Humanities at San Diego City College. She has a Master's Degree from the University of Chicago and a Ph.D. from the University of California at Davis.